KRESKIN'S MIND POWER BOOK

USE YOUR HEAD TO GET AHEAD!
WITH

KRESKIN'S MIND POWER BOOK

BY KRESKIN

McGRAW-HILL BOOK COMPANY

NEW YORK   ST. LOUIS   SAN FRANCISCO   DÜSSELDORF
LONDON   MEXICO   SYDNEY   TORONTO

Book design by Lynn Braswell.

Illustrations by Edine Podell.

1 2 3 4 5 6 7 8 9 0 DODO 7 8 3 2 1 0 9 8 7

Library of Congress Cataloging in Publication Data

Kreskin, date
Kreskin's mind power book.
1. Intellect. 2. Success. I. Title.
II. Title: Mind power book.
BF431.K67   158'.1   77-24545
ISBN 0-07-035480-4

To Lou Reda — my personal manager,
with whom I've had no written contract — but simply
a bond of true friendship and an awareness
of his limitless faith in my abilities.

CONTENTS

INTRODUCTION

The writing of this book has been a dream of mine for more than a decade. Much of its content—the techniques for personal improvement—has been proved to me during my career—both in my public appearances as a lecturer-entertainer and in my private practice as a consultant to physicians, dentists, psychologists, and law enforcement agencies dealing with cases amenable to my background and experience in tapping the mind's inner potential. (For eight years I held an office in East Orange, New Jersey, with Dr. Harold Hansen, a clinical psychologist, who would refer patients to me whom he felt could benefit from my techniques.)

In my performances I have dramatized and demonstrated the often remarkable mentality untapped by most people; in my private consultations I have personally trained people in the use of mind power techniques for their own self-improvement.

I am not a "hypnotist," nor has hypnotism been associated with my work for many years. The reason for my dropping such an association should be made. It gradually became evident to me through the years that you do not have to be "hypnotized" in order to accomplish dramatic deeds through your thought processes. Indeed, everything that can be accomplished with a person under "hypnosis" can be done without the "trance" state. The key—imagination! The imagination can be a powerful force in your life providing you are strongly motivated and will practice stimulating your imagination through suggestion.

As a footnote to my burying the "hypnotic trance," I should point out that numerous behavior scientists, including research psychologist Dr. T. X. Barber of Medfield, Mass., have tried to find an objective, physiological index of hypnosis such as change in brain waves, pulse, respiration, or electrical conductance of skin. To date, no one has been able to demonstrate any physiological measure of changes. In fact, there is no way of distinguishing a hypnotic subject from a person who is normally awake.

Because there is at this point in the history of science absolutely no hard-core evidence of a special hypnotic state, I recently offered, in a public press conference, $50,000 to anyone who could conclusively prove the existence of such a trance under controlled test conditions. To date, no scientist, doctor, or psychologist has come forth. In general, researchers and "experts" have tended to overlook the patterns of thinking that can enable you to tap your greater potential.

It became obvious to me early in my career that there has been a serious need to communicate the techniques of mental discipline and mind conditioning to the general public. Dr. Norman Vincent Peale once commented before an audience of mine in Rome, Italy, "What Kreskin is doing is really not very mysterious. All he is doing is dramatizing what I've preached in my writings for years." Dr. Peale and numerous others have written for years on the power of positive thinking. Movements have come and gone dealing basically with the power of thought. When these fads have passed, the one common denominator remains true—the power of suggestion. It is time that the power of suggestion be stripped of its mysteries, whether it be oversimplification to meaningless alpha states (which have nothing directly to do with the subject's accomplishment) to TM (whose adherents make ludicrous claims of invisibility and the skill of "flying"). The power of mental suggestion and its potential has had many put-downs—from "mystical claptrap" to "a form of hypnosis." But it is simply and unquestionably the basis of mind expansion and life enhancement. This book is based on my firm belief in suggestion. It is not psychic phenomena, nor science fiction, nor a pop system put together for a growing demand for self-help "magic." This is not a magic book. It is a program of practical approaches which should enable you to find keys for improving and expanding your mental potential. This improvement can cover the entire range of life skills from athletics, to studies, to personal and business relations. Yet it is not a book of self-healing or psychotherapy.

Perhaps no one can completely tap all resources and potentials in one lifetime. I am giving you, however, the keys which can unlock the door to a continual program of self-development and improvement. What I ask of you is a commitment. You may not use every technique in this book. But you will find a direction, through those techniques which work best for you. In time they will become automatic. You will find yourself achieving a knack for responding to your own constructive suggestion or idea, with less and less conscious effort. You will then have the tools you will need to apply your mind power techniques to life's challenges. In time the positive suggestion and conditioning approach will reflect itself in your work and play and in a life style which I believe will bring you greater happiness, a sense of achievement, and an inner serenity.

I wish you the most positive thoughts.

Kreskin

□ 1 □

CONCENTRATION
Your First Key
To Success

Concentration is the most vital factor in developing the powers of the inner mind. With it, you can accomplish seeming miracles; without it, progress in mind control will be minimal. There is no reason to doubt your ability to develop this faculty if you follow the right procedures, as you will begin to discover within the next few pages.

□ CONCENTRATION PROCEDURES □

Here is a good definition of concentration: "the focusing of the entire being at a given moment upon a central point of interest, either inward or outward, as required." An excellent analogy is an amateur photographer taking a picture. His mind is centered on both the subject and the object, which includes distance, lighting, posing, and—most of all—catching everything "at a given moment."

All forms of concentration demand a consideration of details along with personalized action. This means that to concentrate, you must be alert. Many "experts" have nevertheless mistakenly recommended a completely opposite course. They ask you to look at an uncommonly bright object, or even a common object like a key or a pencil, and give it your sole attention, noting its most minute details while eliminating all other thoughts from your mind, so you can apply full mental effort toward one aim alone.

That is not concentration. It is a form of fixation, specifically "fixation of attention," which is practically a mental dead end. As you continue the process, you may become susceptible to outside suggestions such as sounds or voices (particularly the latter) that penetrate your growing drowsiness. You may respond to them or you may not; in either case, once the outside stimulus has either ceased or faded, your tendency is to fall asleep.

□ CONCENTRATION VERSUS FIXATION □

True concentration, in its fullest sense, consists of focusing the mind on an idea, rather than merely fixing attention on a physical object. By doing this you can adhere to your initial purpose, which is to eliminate outside distractions while endeavoring to draw deep-set suggestions from your own inner mind. Some authorities have likened the concentration process to the drilling of an oil well, which, though a commonplace action in itself, can bring highly productive results.

Remember, however, that some preliminary training is essential for effective concentration. You can start with what would ordinarily be mere fixation, with tiring results, except that in this case you make it purposeful and therefore more meaningful. As a brief preliminary test, it will serve the added function of acquainting you with the difference between the futility of fixation and the purpose of applied concentration.

□ THE REPEATED READING PROCESS □

For your first phase, use an uninteresting book, bland and childish. Open to a random page. Start at the top and read steadily down to the bottom. Start again at the top and read down just as you did before. Repeat this, time after time, for a period of five to ten minutes or longer, depending on your customary reading speed. Keep on until it is tiring, to complete the fixation process; then shut your eyes and review what you have read. It will naturally mean no more than at the start, emphasizing the futility of simple fixation.

For the second phase, take a page from a volume of technical or scholarly material; read it and reread it. With each reading, try to absorb some important information or improve your interpretation of what you have read before; that is, maintain a progressive purpose throughout. This too can prove tiring, but when you relax and try to recall what you have read, you may find yourself adding points you overlooked before or seeking answers to queries that have just occurred to you. Either way, you are drawing from your inner mind, the great aim of the concentration process.

□ BASIC EXERCISES IN CONCENTRATION □

Here are some techniques for making a transition from fixation to concentration, each rendering you amenable to suggestions of varying degree. You will notice that in both phases of the Repeated Reading Process you first gave *attention* to material in a book, then you added *interest* by reading through the material, and you finished with *repetition* by going over it, time after time, thus conforming to the routine described as the AIR (Attention, Interest, and Repetition) formula.

Only after continued repetition did your attention begin to lag, and interest soon faded. Repetition became a purely mechanical process, causing your original effort at concentration to dwindle to a point of mere fixation. With the first test, this happened fairly soon, because the material was trite. What you needed was some new factor to recapture your attention, to provide interest deep enough that it would not be dulled by added repetition.

You gained that through reading material of a more advanced type, which demanded a greater amount of concentration. This forestalled fixation for a longer period, until interest again began a fade-out, producing the same result. Superficially, it might seem that this could be overcome by simply moving into higher brackets of reading material that would further rouse your attention and place greater demands on your concentration, but such is not the case.

You have probably seen people go to sleep while they were reading; you may have done so yourself. The same applies to movies and television or, even worse, driving a car. It is simply that excessive repetition induces fixation as the only possible escape from a situation in which concentration itself can provide no further stimulus. Therefore, you must concentrate on a definite objective to attain the desired state of concentration. The following exercises are specifically for this purpose.

CLOCK-WATCHING

For best results, use an electric clock with a large second hand that sweeps around the dial, although one with a smaller second hand will do. A watch with a second hand will also do, especially one of the "sweep" type.

Step One: Place the clock (or watch) where you can study it closely; then read the instructions carefully, so you can follow them step by step without losing track of what you are to do.

Set the hour and minute hands at exactly twelve o'clock so they will not interfere with your watching the second hand move around the dial.

Step Two: Wait until the second hand has reached the twelve-o'clock position; then, as a preliminary test, let your eyes follow its trip around the dial until you tire or lose interest. Note how many seconds it took for that to happen.

Step Three: Take a brief rest; then repeat the experiment, trying to carry it further. You will probably find it almost impossible to keep your thoughts from wandering during the brief time span of a single minute.

Step Four: Keep repeating this as a regular exercise and you will notice a steady improvement. Be sure to take sufficient rest periods. You are not out to set an endurance record, but to develop your power of concentration. This is better than confining your attention to a fixed object, as the motion of the second hand carries your *attention* along with it, while your *interest* in reaching the minute mark encourages you to *repeat* the exercise under identical conditions.

Step Five: To develop the AIR formula further, focus your attention on the seconds themselves, by counting them off mentally, as the hand goes around the dial. This added *attention* creates new *interest,* inviting extra *repetition.*

Step Six: Continue this synchronized action at intervals until you find you can reach the minute mark without distraction. Continue the exercise; increase up to two minutes, or longer if you wish.

Step Seven: Having established a suitable limit, repeat this exercise whenever you want to concentrate on some special subject. This exercise itself combined the AIR principles to a degree that should keep you alert to *whatever comes to mind.*

Note that this exercise counteracts fixation in two ways: (1) it focuses your gaze on a moving object; (2) it keeps your mind geared to the action by timing it as you go along. It is not necessary to count off the seconds as you watch the moving hand. It automatically checks them on the dial as it comes to them. However, to keep your counting uniform, you can use a catch phrase such as "One second one"—"one second one"—"one second one," timing these repeats to the exact speed of the hand as it marks off the seconds. This conditions your mind for the next exercise in concentration.

THE MENTAL TIME COUNT

Among other things, this technique enables you to tell time with your eyes closed, which is of double value in concentration since it eliminates any visual distractions. However, it is best to start your preliminary exercise with your eyes wide open as you can then shift directly from Clock-Watching into the Mental Time Count.

Step One: Count off seconds, timing them by the second hand of a clock or watch, using the phrase "one second one" to keep them uniform. Limit this to groups of ten seconds: for example, when the second hand hits 20, time it from there to 30; then pick it up again from 40 to 50; then from 10 to 20.

Step Two: Now vary your catch phrase as you go along, making it "one second one"—"one second two"—"one second three"—"one second four"—"one second five"—"one second six"—"one second seven"—"one second eight"—"one second nine"—"one second TEN." As you repeat this, you can close your eyes to start, then open them on TEN, checking the clock to see how close you came.

Step Three: Continue the "ten count" until you are sure of it. Here you are combining *attention* to the individual numbers with *interest* in hitting exactly on the mark of TEN and *repetition* as the means of achieving it. Thus the AIR formula will be working at full strength when you go into:

Step Four: Here you extend your count. When you reach TEN, keep your eyes closed and *repeat the count* taking TWENTY as a new goal, so it will run: "one second one"—"one second two"—"one second three"—"one second four"—"one second five"—"one second six"—"one second seven"—"one second eight"—"one second nine"—eventually to "one second TWENTY." With that, open your eyes to see how well you did.

Step Five: Once you are reaching TWENTY right on time, you can extent your count to THIRTY, then to FORTY and FIFTY, finally taking SIXTY as your target. In testing your ability at higher numbers, you should always start when the second hand hits the 60-second mark, so you can check the clock exactly when you open your eyes at the finish of the count.

Step Six: Practice this count for proficiency, always remembering to count each group from 1 to 10, to keep the syllables uniform, finishing each group with TEN, TWENTY, and so on, so your final count will be "one second SIXTY." If you want to stretch it to two minutes, start the next minute with "two seconds one"—"two seconds two"—"two seconds three," and so on up to "two seconds SIXTY." That will keep reminding you that you are working on *Minute Two;* you can do the same with *Minute Three,* and so forth.

Like Clock-Watching, this exercise is flexible, having the same kind of mobility that induces concentration and makes the mind alert. It can also be put to practical use, such as checking time while waiting for planes, trains, or buses, keeping appointments, or checking the time on long-distance phone calls. The more you practice the Mental Time Count, the more valuable you will find it.

Many futile attempts at concentration date back to the old technique of "counting sheep" in order to go to sleep. People counted an endless procession of nonexistent sheep jumping over imaginary fences, hoping they would fall asleep through sheer boredom. Today, many people give up after fifty or sixty sheep and take a sleeping pill instead, for "sheep-counting" is not actually a form of concentration, but merely a mild type of fixation.

The same applies to other forms of counting that just keep going on and on. Take counting to a thousand as an example. Before you reach a few hundred, you have overtaxed your attention and lost interest—and there is nothing to be gained through such repetition. In short, you will have deflated the AIR formula completely. You will be skipping some numbers, losing count of others, and approaching a state of confusion rather than concentration.

Nothing can be gained by reducing the count, so the only course is to extend it, which sounds even worse, unless you shoot for something that will capture your imagination. Instead of a mere thousand, why not make it a million? Or, better still, a billion? Or even a trillion!

The idea itself demands attention and certainly should arouse interest if repetition can be brought within meaningful bounds. All that is possible through:

THE FAR-OUT COUNT

■ OVERALL PURPOSE: Keep this fact in mind: You are going to count steadily and methodically to a total far beyond all normal limitations. You will include all necessary enumerations, so it will be possible to check back and prove that you were entirely correct. To speed the process and make it feasible, you will simply eliminate all unnecessary repetition.

Step One: Slowly, emphatically, count the digits: "1–2–3–4–5–6–7–8–9–10." Repeat TEN for emphasis and count by tens: "10–20–30–40–50–60–70–80–90–100." Again emphasize: ONE HUNDRED. Continue by hundreds: "100–200–300–400–500–600–700–800–900–1000." You have reached your original objective: ONE THOUSAND. Mentally picture it as 1000.

Step Two: Continue your count by thousands: 1000–2000–3000–4000–5000–6000–7000–8000–9000–TEN THOUSAND. Repeat that number as you continue by tens of thousands: 10,000–20,000–up to ONE HUNDRED THOUSAND. From there, continue with 100,000–200,000– to your next objective: ONE MILLION. Mentally picture it as 1,000,000.

Step Three: From here you count by millions: 1 million–2 million–3 million–4 million–5 million–6 million–7 million–8 million–9 million–TEN MILLION. From there, count by tens of millions: 10 million–20 million– until you reach 100 million–200 million– to your further objective: ONE BILLION. Mentally picture it as 1,000,000,000.

Step Four: Now you can count in terms of billions: 1 billion–2 billion–3 billion– up to TEN BILLION. From there, count by tens of billions until you reach 100 billion. From there, you continue by hundreds of billions up to your final objective: ONE TRILLION. Picture it as 1,000,000,000,000.

Step Five: Let your impressions catch up with you as you dwell on that staggering total. Just reeling off those increasing figures produces a floating feeling that in terms of mileage could be applied to space travel, carrying past the moon, beyond the limits of the solar system, and on your way to Alpha Centauri, the nearest star. In dollars, you could fancy yourself a millionaire, then find yourself thinking of the national debt and later the wealth of all the world. From such beginnings, you go into:

Step Six: Here you let all those impressions crystallize, forming visual images of your own. Chances are, they will bring you down to earth, confronting you with problems but at the same time offering solutions. Or your flight of fancy may have carried you so far out of this world that you now find yourself beyond all trivial worries. Try it and see!

■ NOTE: Although your fanciful count has been numerically adequate, you have reached the trillion mark in the time it would take to count to 120 in standard fashion. So there is no need to hurry it; in fact, after you have tried it a few times, you may want to prolong it, which you can, by continuing on from a trillion to a quadrillion, a quintillion, a sextillion, a septillion, an octillion, a nonillion, or a decillion—1,000,000,-000,000,000,000,000,000,000,000,000.

□ 2 □

VISUAL IMAGERY
How to Develop It through Concentration

Having now applied the basic rules of simple concentration, you have crossed the threshold into visual imagery, or "thinking in pictures" while developing ideas through the inner mind. Ordinarily, these images are simply incidental to the concentration process. To bring them into full focus, you need a stimulus in the form of visual imagery that carries over from one phase to another and may eventually reach the higher stage of imagination. This in turn leads to inspiration.

Mental imagery is easily invoked through the power of suggestion. Nearly two centuries ago, Friedrich Anton Mesmer proved this when he touched the members of a group with a wand, causing them to imagine they were magnetized to such an extent that they acted as though experiencing electric shocks. Because of their faith in Mesmer and his prestige, each person's action caused others to imitate it; that was all. Today, when I tell an entire audience to clasp their hands and then try to separate them—which they can't! —I am demonstrating that same power of suggestion, applied to the mass mind. Individuals, witnessing the reactions of others, picture themselves in the same state. They just won't let themselves out of their own bind until they are told that they can do so.

It doesn't take a superforce to sway the mass mind. All people need is someone to trigger the reaction and they will do the rest themselves. This was evidenced by the community spirit back in the horse-and-buggy days before automobiles and airplanes began taking people far from home. Quilting parties, clambakes, hayrides, square dances, taffy pulls, and round songs were the order of the day. Anybody could suggest one and everybody else would fall in line, because it was easy for them to picture themselves at such functions.

When they were there, they gave themselves whole-heartedly to the thing at hand and forgot other matters for the time being. I mention "round songs" in particular, because when a group of people sang in unison, they had to keep both music and words in mind, a form of mental imagery. As an example, take the song that went:

> Forty-nine bottles, hanging on a wall,
> Forty-nine bottles, hanging on a wall,
> Take one bottle from them all—
> Forty-eight bottles, hanging on a wall.

The next verse began with "Forty-eight bottles" and ended with "Forty-seven"; next with "Forty-seven," ending with "Forty-six," and so on down the line, with the last verse starting "Just one bottle hanging on a wall" and ending "There aren't any bottles hanging on a wall." While singing all those verses, the group would become so intense that a troop of elephants could have tramped by without being noticed. At the finish, the singers would shake hands and slap one another's backs as though they had done something wonderful. And, for the moment, they really thought they had, because their minds had reached such a high pitch that they could practically see those bottles going one by one.

As a modern equivalent of that scene, picture a group of people watching a television screen during a countdown prior to the blastoff of a space ship. Intensity grows as the seconds decrease, until the big moment when the suspense of the countdown shifts to the action of the takeoff (which develops a suspense of its own, since there is always a chance that something may go wrong).

Note that each of these examples—the round song and the countdown—represents a form of objective concentration and therefore comes under the heading of fixation as applied to the conscious mind, although visual imagery can be introduced as an added feature. However, if you keep picturing bottles and subtracting them one by one, your mind will be so occupied with the procedure that you will find yourself absolutely nowhere when you get down to zero.

Similarly, if you keep picturing a spacecraft waiting for a takeoff all during your mental countdown, your mood will simply be one of continued expectation that reverses itself at blastoff; as the rocket zooms off through outer space, it will leave you right where you started. With either process, you might find yourself highly susceptible to outside suggestions after concentrating in such a fashion. But you will have done nothing to stir the working of your inner consciousness, which is the real purpose of all mind expansion.

The way to accomplish mind expansion is to use the "countdown" purely as a mechanical device (like a timer) that accompanies a visualization procedure of your own creation. This results in a form of actual accomplishment that brings your unconscious or subjective impressions to the surface, so that you can immediately apply them to a conscious, objective purpose.

Highly effective toward building inner interest as well as sustaining it is the following.

REVERSE COUNT VISUALIZATION

Step One: Read through the instructions that follow, thus programming yourself for the steps as detailed.

Step Two: Close your eyes and tilt your head slightly backward, as if gazing toward an object just above your usual eye level.

Step Three: Visualize a flame burning on the wick of a lighted candle, wavering as you watch it.

Step Four: Keeping this primary fixation outlined in your mind, take three long, steady breaths.

Step Five: Now, breathe easily, naturally, and as you exhale, mentally pronounce the number 50.

Step Six: Continue your natural breathing, counting down as you exhale each breath: 49–48–47–46–45–44–43–42–41–40." During the count, keep picturing the wavering flame, with the upper portion of the candle softening from the heat.

Step Seven: Continue the breathing count: "39–38–37–36–35–34–33–32–31–30." As you count, picture a blob of wax detaching itself from the rim of the candle and trickling slowly down the side, then another—and another—about one to every third count.

Step Eight: Continue the count: "29–28–27–26–25–24–23–22–21–20." The blobs are trickling faster, one for every other count, and the candle is decreasing in size with them.

Step Nine: Continue the count: "19–18–17–16–15–14–13–12–11–10." A blob with each count, with the candle melting so rapidly that you can see its base with the melted wax piled about it.

Step Ten: While counting "9–8–7–6–5–4–3–2–1–" picture the molten mass spreading like a pancake, with the candle flame dwindling down into the center more rapidly than your count.

Step Eleven: With the count of "Zero" the candle flame is extinguished, blacking out the entire picture. Take five deep breaths while keeping your eyes closed to appreciate the utter blackness.

Step Twelve: Pause, keeping your eyes closed, and wait for random thoughts to develop, either as pictures or inward impressions.

This procedure serves the double purpose of draining away outer thoughts through concentration and leaving a void that automatically draws up inner impressions. How vivid they are depends a great deal on the individual, but even more on practice: It takes a certain knack as well as experience to appreciate the full possibilities of this system. Having already tried the simpler concentration tests, particularly the Mental Time Count, you should be somewhat preconditioned for Reverse Count Visualization, but don't take too much for granted at the start.

Counting down from fifty to zero requires some care, while timing it to the melting wax demands still more concentration, which is exactly what you are seeking. If your mind becomes distracted, do not force yourself to come back to the subject matter. Rather, be aware of the fact that the material, the ideas, and the autosuggestions still can work effectively. The important thing is not to worry about the distractions. If the distractions come, if you missed the count, or if you have trouble with the visualization, as long as you don't worry about it and continue calmly on with the exercise, the effects can be almost the same. If you miss the count, go in the wrong direction, or lose place, you should continue; somewhere along the line, you will come back, even if it is not at the same position; that is not important. What is especially important is that you not allow distractions or losing place to seem a problem. Instead of stopping and beginning all over again, you should continue calmly, and not worry. Also be careful to avoid anticipation during the countdown. Don't think ahead to zero or picture the candle melted before you get there. Just take everything in order, adhering to the routine described.

Naturally, this requires practice—or a better term would be *rehearsal,* since in a sense you are putting on a dramatic act of your own making. Try it at intervals during the day, picking times when you can relax, free from disturbing influences. A comfortable chair in a quiet room would be ideal, but you can adapt yourself to less favorable conditions. A reclining position is excellent, with your head tilted upward; so is lying down (face upward, so as to visualize the lighted candle standing upright).

You may gain some immediate results from this countdown procedure, but don't expect too much too soon. You are conditioning yourself in the art of gradually eliminating a preconceived image so that another will evolve; in short, you will be experiencing a transition from the known into the unknown. It may take two weeks of three practice sessions daily before you are able to relax to the point where the countdown and the melting process blend automatically. Even when they do, it is a good plan to continue the practice sessions to avoid lapsing back into earlier stages where tension was apt to hinder concentration.

As you proceed, you may find you are losing count or that the candle is melting too slowly or too rapidly. Neither matters, because you can shift from one to the other, picking up the count at where you think it should be, slowing it or speeding it to keep pace with the melting candle. You are not timing yourself during this procedure; your real aim is to synchronize two factors—counting and melting—bringing them to a climax at zero. With practice, you will forget or ignore that target until you are almost there.

□ ALTERNATIVE FORMS OF □
REVERSE COUNT

Before going into case histories demonstrating the final results of this procedure, some alternative forms of the Reverse Count system should be considered. The choice of a candle flame as a focal image is logical, because one time-honored method of inducing fixation is to have a person gaze at an actual candle flame instead of a bright object or an electric light. The wavering of a candle builds attention into interest, like the motion of a second hand on a clock. However, both can prove tiring through too much repetition. That is not the case with an imaginary candle flame. You can fancy yourself watching one flicker incessantly without tiring your eyes at all, since you are keeping them shut, but this can become boring. For those who would like something more spectacular, we recommend:

THE ABOMINABLE SNOWMAN

You have probably heard of the Abominable Snowman, a gigantic apelike creature that is said to haunt the blizzard-swept slopes of the Himalaya Mountains, but you don't have to envision such a monster for this test. Your snowman can be the backyard variety, the kind kids make by rolling three snowballs and piling them up to represent legs, body, and a head which they decorate with a crude face and top with an old hat.

With this in mind, proceed as follows:

Step One: Read through the instructions.

Step Two: Gaze toward a window or glance briefly at a light; then close your eyes and tilt your head backward, as if viewing an object above normal eye level.

Step Three: Visualize the face of your snowman against a sunlit background; the funnier the face the better. Even let it grimace as you watch it.

Step Four: Take at least five deep breaths. Try to sense the warmth of the sunny background.

Step Five: Start your count with 50 and immediately follow with "49–48–47–" and so on, slowly, still concentrating on the sun's intensity.

Step Six: Picture the snowman's head beginning to melt; then the body, slumping slowly down toward the feet. Concentrate on this more than the count as the latter nears the 30 mark.

Step Seven: The entire form is becoming a spreading mass of melted snow. If you have lost count, it doesn't matter. Pick it up anywhere, say "9–8–7–6–"

Step Eight: As you reach zero, every vestige of the snowman is completely gone. All that is left is a white background.

Step Nine: Breathe deeply, counting from 1 up to 5 with each breath. Open your eyes and wait for inner impressions to develop.

A comparison of the methods just described will show that each has certain advantages worthy of careful consideration. With the candle flame as a focal point, some people gain an immediate visualization, not necessarily of a bright flame but at least of an outline that suffices. Even without such a start, you may find it easy to imagine what a wavering candle flame would look like. This can work well in a completely darkened room, hence no outside stimulus is necessary as a starter. The count must usually be emphasized, however, to time the melting process exactly.

With the snowman as a basis, the situation is just the opposite. You are picturing a sunlit outdoor scene, so you need daylight or artificial illumination as a stimulus before closing your eyes to gain the best results. A good way to form a strong mental outline of the snowman is to picture a group of boys rolling big snowballs and piling them up to form the snowman. When the melting begins, it will take over completely, with the countdown becoming incidental until the finish.

Various people to whom I have described this melting process have tried their own mode of visualization with excellent results. Instead of picturing a snowman, you can imagine yourself far at sea, slowly approaching a distant iceberg that looms larger as you near it. To compensate for this, the iceberg begins to melt more rapidly than your approach, so that it is entirely gone when you reach it, leaving only a watery background to receive impressions from your inner mind. If you prefer to work on a smaller scale, picture a bowl or carton filled with ice cubes that begin melting with your countdown, or even a dish of ice cream, which also melts while you watch it, leaving a soupy background.

This brings color into your mental picture—chocolate, strawberry, or pistachio—and you may even taste one of those flavors during the process. My own favorite method for gaining complete mental relaxation and bringing deep-down impressions to the surface involves color only.

Step One: Read the instructions and choose one of the three procedures (a, b, or c) listed below; then use it as your pattern.

Step Two: Assume a comfortable position, either seated, reclining, or lying down.

Step Three: Half-closing your eyes, imagine yourself enjoying complete relaxation in an environment of a simple but specific type:

a. A sandy beach, looking toward the ocean or a great lake, with a clear sky above.

b. A grassy bank in summertime, with a verdant background and trees furnishing a comfortable shade.

c. A fireplace with crackling logs providing a welcome blaze following a hike through wintry snow.

Step Four: Closing your eyes entirely, concentrate on an appropriate color:

a. Blue, representing the water and the sky above, in varying shades.

b. Green, representing grass and foliage.

c. Various colors suggested by the flicker of flames and glow of embers.

Step Five: Take five deep breaths and begin a downward count from 50 to zero, continually imagining yourself becoming absorbed or even engulfed amid a sea of color.

Step Six: At zero, take five deep breaths and open your eyes.

This is primarily an exercise in relaxation, as you will readily learn when you open your eyes at zero and look around. To some people it is almost like finding themselves in a new world. That is all the more reason why it should be used as an advanced form of concentration to develop impressions emanating from the inner mind. This exercise brings us to the crux of visual imagery.

Some people can actually see colors when they close their eyes, particularly on a bright day or in a strong light, but this is not necessary in color visualization. All you have to do is think in terms of a color and you will find that it tends to form in your mind. My favorites are blue and green, as both are restful and natural. Thus, in using either of the first two formulas you will find yourself comparing shades of that particular color, even if it does not actually form.

With *a* you can contrast the deep blue of the sea and the bright blue of the sky, with the horizon as a dividing line, or you can think of a parade featuring navy-blue uniforms and gray-blue pennants. With *b* you can think of the bright-green leaves of maple trees against a background of dark evergreens or the green of a grassy bank reflected in a limpid stream. If shades fail to develop, simply repeat the word *blue* or *green* while thinking of the scene that goes with that particular color.

With *c* you have two choices: One is to picture the crackling firelight with its ever-changing hues, even sensing its all-pervading warmth, or you can focus upon whatever color finally becomes predominant, from dwindling yellow flame to deep red embers. Again, you don't have to *see* the colors; just imagine that they are *there*. It is the *idea* that counts.

□ PRESETTING YOUR MIND—CONTEMPLATION □

Practice the reverse count exercise three times a day for a week or two, in order to familiarize yourself with a particular time span by the backward count. This is the key to the ultimate exercise: presetting your mind. Just before you take the five deep breaths, picture mentally what seems most natural or effective—a color, snowman, candle, fireplace, etc. Now, with your eyes closed, take five deep breaths, hold the fifth, exhale and relax. Don't consciously count, or force the image; simply allow whatever image you've decided upon to flow into your mind. Remembering how long it previously took to count from 50 to zero, you will simply sense the time is now up. Then count from one to five and open your eyes. At the end of a week of practice you may reset in your mind some idea which could set off a chain of thought during the period when you used to count from 50 to zero. Capsulize the thought in one or two words, or in a single mental picture, or even in a feeling: a new job, choosing your major in college, a loved one, taking a trip on a gliding boat, or the humming of your car, etc.

□ FROM IDEAS TO ACTUALITIES □

The term *chain of thought* is more than a catch phrase. Any sequence of thoughts is necessarily formed from a series of links, which ordinarily represent conscious observations or impressions, with occasional dips into the unconscious. Picture a man in his home workshop, carefully fitting parts for a model he is constructing. Each of his thoughts falls into a logical, conscious procession, just like the pattern he is following, until the shrill blare of a fire siren comes from the street.

All thoughts of the model are obliterated from that man's mind. He finds himself out in the front yard, meeting a neighbor carrying a brush from a paint job he was doing. Simultaneously they blurt the same question: "Where's the fire?," and with that as a common denominator, both begin a completely new chain of conscious thought impressions stemming from the sudden emergency, completely obliterating the original sequences already in progress.

□ APPLICATION TO THE SUBCONSCIOUS □

Through the exercises given so far, your mind can break a conscious thought chain as effectively as a fire signal. The deeper you dip into the unconscious, the more immune you become to outside suggestions, until you find yourself almost entirely dependent on the dictates of your inner consciousness.

That is when you should follow the new thought train and

see where it leads you. Don't look for images right away; stay with ideas as they develop, but any time an idea asserts itself as an image, you will know that the trail is getting hot. Every time you surprise yourself by scoring what may seem a trifling hit, you will be on the way to something bigger, though it may seem a long way off.

I learned this through my own experience. I was so confident that the power of suggestion would bring results I kept on trying long after someone else would have given up. Finally I reached the stage where I could just sit back and relax, letting everything melt away until new ideas developed themselves into actualities. Then I knew that the same technique could be used by others, except that they didn't realize it, because they hadn't sustained the method long enough.

I have constantly encouraged people to keep repeating these exercises until they become habit. Having learned to clear their minds of extraneous thoughts, they will be able to concentrate on the follow-through. Whatever develops should be analyzed and taken as a starting point to a new and productive thought chain.

HOW ONE MAN TURNED PASSIVITY INTO ACTIVITY

■ CASE 1. Dick Harwood was an insurance salesman who had hit a run of bad luck. He would start the day enthusiastically, but if he failed to sell a prospect on one of his first few calls, he would become discouraged. This made him jittery in his approach to others and, even worse, he became impatient if anyone kept him waiting for an interview. A night's sleep usually restored his enthusiastic mood, but it seldom lasted until noon the next day. When he came to the point of taking whole days off rather than face unreceptive clients, Dick realized that he had to do something.

So he took up concentration and tried the countdown

system, just to "keep his cool," as he put it. After each futile call, he would sit in his car and go through the melting process until he had cleared his mind of thoughts of failure. If he had to wait in an outside office, he repeated the same procedure, which completely curbed his former impatience. He no longer worried about losing his prospects; they were always glad to welcome him and seldom kept him waiting, for he was always in a pleasant, receptive mood. But he was faced by the same problem that had given him the jitters and forced him to find the cure: He still wasn't selling insurance.

Previously he had been a go-getter, the symbol of outward activity, which overcame sales resistance from his prospects, as he termed his potential customers. By switching to outward passivity, he had reversed the situation. There was no resistance on the part of the prospective buyer; it wasn't needed, because there was no longer any pressure from the would-be seller.

Dick Harwood didn't realize this. He no longer griped because nobody was buying insurance from him; instead, he wondered why he wasn't selling it. His friends tried to give him new leads. But he was intent on just holding his own, he was barely able to hang onto his job. Then the crisis came.

He had clinched a big deal that depended on a merger of two companies and was waiting for his man to come back from the meeting and sign the insurance applications. Dick went through the melting process while he waited in his car; not once or twice, but three times. At the end of the third routine, his mind was so completely cleared that it suddenly began to swell with new impressions. Dick saw himself tucking the signed policies in his pocket and driving out of town along a road he had never taken before, as if celebrating a triumph.

The president of the company returned and Dick was ushered into the office to hear the news. It consisted of a friendly handshake and the president's announcement: "Too bad, Dick, but the merger is off." All Dick could do was smile it off in the amiable way that he had acquired through his exercises in concentration. Back in his car, Dick calmed himself with another countdown. At the finish, his mind formed the same impression of that lonely road, but even more vividly than before.

Instead of returning to the office or calling on other clients, Dick decided to drive home by another route. He had only gone a few miles when he came to a bridge that was closed for repairs, forcing him to take a detour along a wooded stream. A mile later, he saw a detour arrow pointing to the right, but the road to the left bore a sign that said GLENWOOD. That rang a bell in Dick's mind. Weeks before, a friend had suggested that he look up a man named Clausen who lived in Glenwood, but Dick never bothered to follow up such leads—he was having enough trouble selling insurance to his own prospects, so it seemed foolish to start canvassing strangers.

This situation, though, was different; not because Dick regarded Mr. Clausen as a likely customer, but because the road to Glenwood reminded him of the one that he had pictured while waiting in his car expecting to make a big sale that didn't come through. He took the road to Glenwood and found that the town consisted chiefly of a large, old-fashioned building which bore the sign H. J. CLAUSEN, GENERAL STORE. Dick went in and introduced himself, deciding that he could at least make up for wasted time by buying some groceries to take home.

He found Mr. Clausen in a buying mood. Their mutual friend had told him to expect a "live wire" who would give him much-needed advice on insurance of all kinds. Mr. Clausen needed it, because he did a big business with people in a nearby resort area that was expanding so rapidly that Clausen had decided to expand too. Dick wound up having dinner with Clausen at one of the resort hotels and he headed home with orders for more insurance than he'd hoped to get from the merger that didn't come through.

Dick realized then that he'd gotten into a groove. The fault lay with his prospects, not with himself. Through repeated concentration, his inner mind had provided him with passive acceptance of his problem; but that was only the halfway mark. It was when he pushed the process further that his inner mind began to activate his purposes with positive results.

This case can be multiplied by dozens. Dick's urge to do things his own way made him reject all other suggestions. But he didn't dismiss them entirely; he just buried them, like a well-fed dog with a bone it doesn't need. Dick had been a victim of his own fixations. But when his unconscious had stored enough power to provide its own suggestion, he had only to tap it through intensive introspection.

From that one experience, Dick applied the inner system constantly. From then on, he didn't just clear his conscious mind and go back to the same old grind. He waited until his inner thoughts took over. His mind would flash back to some chance conversation, and he would find himself heeding advice to which he wouldn't have even listened before. Or he would wait for some new vista to develop; instead of consciously picturing himself waiting in somebody's office, he would visualize a friend congratulating him on a fine drive he had just made from a tee on his favorite golf course, which promptly took top place on his agenda for that afternoon.

If new leads developed as a result, fine. If not, Dick still had the satisfaction of shaking off the shackles that had been weighing him down to the point where they dominated his whole way of life. Check a list of your own friends and you may find that many of them are so hidebound by their own conscious minds that only a dip into the unconscious can release them. That, in turn, may enable you to tap some of your own hidden resources through a similar program.

In sharp contrast to the numerous cases where it takes inner imagery to break the bonds of outward frustration are those where smug satisfaction can undo an overabundance of conscious effort. Examples of these are also quite plentiful, but are usually overlooked because things apparently have gone so well that improvement seems unnecessary. The best way to appreciate this is to cite an example and apply the findings to other cases later.

■ CASE 2. Larry Burrick was a technical writer for a conglomerate that paid its staff well but was very exacting in its demands. That suited Larry. He liked details and could outwork anyone else in the shop. Whenever other staff writers became overproud of their achievements, the higher-ups had a habit of comparing their work to Larry's, much to his credit and not theirs. That didn't make Larry too popular with his fellow writers, but he didn't mind that. It only increased his confidence in his own ability. To silence his critics, he became eager to prove the point.

Larry's opportunity came when the management decided to produce a massive history of the corporation's mergers and expansions. This was scheduled as a staff project, with various phases to be handled by individual writers. When the directors called on Larry to head the operation, he saw his chance for a grand triumph and offered to take on the entire project personally. Some of the directors balked at letting it become a one-man show, but Larry's ability, knowledge, and seniority enabled him to win his point. Larry knew that he was laying his reputation on the line, but he regarded the challenge as a calculated risk that he could promptly turn to his advantage.

The fact that Larry was already at the top made all the other staff writers happy in the belief that Larry would go on to bigger things and leave the field to them. So they willingly turned over all their data to Larry, who put researchers to work gathering more material which was turned over to a team of typists. As usual, Larry came up with a well-defined, thoroughly documented summary of all the vital facts, with detailed ramifications.

Highly important to the history was the hallowed figure of Ambrose Winsted, who had been president of the parent company for some forty-odd years. To enshrine Winsted further, Larry had his helpers assemble a great array of reports concerning financial transactions, board-meeting reports, formal announcements, and recommendations directly linked to the great man's noteworthy career. With that as a constant theme, the history shaped up to Larry's full satisfaction.

As a technical expert, Larry treated all things objectively. Because he was a stickler for detail, exactitude was his watchword. But once he finished a set task, he became introspective, using recommended exercises to clear his mind of details so that his intensive working hours could be counterbalanced by periods of recreation. By simply closing his eyes and relaxing he was able to direct his conscious mind into a new channel, but it was always one he had planned beforehand; never did he dip into the unconscious beyond the mind-clearing stage. He would review what he had done with satisfaction—but always as fact, not fancy.

Nevertheless, having finished his comprehensive historical outline in which Ambrose Winsted figured so heavily, Larry found it difficult to dismiss Winsted from his mind. He kept seeing a stern-faced portrait of the former president that hung in the board room, staring its disapproval of whatever was going on. When the mental image wouldn't fade, Larry tried to change it and gradually it blurred into another face, which he recognized as that of George Sanville, a writer with whom he had worked years before on a big-city newspaper.

Some time after Larry had taken up technical writing, George had gone into the magazine field and had done quite well.

For the next few days, recollections of George kept stirring in his mind and Larry finally told his secretary to try to locate his old friend. It turned out that George was now publishing a weekly newspaper in his home town. Larry called him up and was relieved to learn that all was going well, for those recurrent thoughts had seemed like a premonition. George, in turn, was pleased to hear from Larry, who told him about the history he was writing. When Larry mentioned the exalted name of Ambrose Winsted, it brought a chuckle over the long-distance wire.

"Ambling Ambrose," laughed George. "That's what they called him from the way he moved around the plant, showing up in places where he was least expected."

That didn't fit Larry's concept of the austere Mr. Winsted. Somewhat indignantly he demanded: "Where did you hear that?"

"From old Ambrose himself," returned George. "He liked the nickname and tried to live up to it. He said the only way to learn what was going on in a department was to drop in on it."

"You mean you really met Ambrose Winsted—"

"Often. I mentioned him in a lot of news articles and did a profile on him for a magazine series. I even have some letters from him, telling what he really thought about certain people. I'll send you copies of the stuff: maybe you can use it."

Thanking George rather bluntly, Larry switched to another subject and terminated the phone call. He had decided to use George's "stuff" as filler for the wastebasket, but changed his mind a few days later, when one of the directors asked to see him privately.

When they were alone, the director told him: "About that

history of yours, Larry. We sent the first draft to some literary critics for advance reactions. Apparently they don't like the way you've treated it."

He handed the reviews to Larry. One said that the history was "written in the style of a telephone book illustrated with blueprints." Another commented that Ambrose Winsted seemed "as alive as an Egyptian mummy just excavated from an ancient tomb." As Larry read the criticisms, the director remarked:

"I'll hold these off until after our next board meeting, Larry. That may give you time to come up with a new approach."

Back in his office, Larry tried to take his mind from his problem by going through his mail. In it were the articles from George. Among letters George had received from Winsted were unpublished photos showing old Ambrose wearing overalls while chatting with workers and pictures taken of him on hunting and fishing trips. On the back of one picture Winsted had scrawled: "They finally changed my nickname from Ambling to Amiable."

That was all Larry needed for his new approach. By taking data from George's articles and putting a team of researchers on the trail once more, he humanized Ambrose Winsted to such an extent that even the conglomerate gained a large share of the reflected glory. Larry's history proved to be a great success, and what impressed him most was the factor that had made it possible. At first, Larry was inclined to attribute it either to sheer coincidence or to some form of extrasensory perception that had linked his mind with George's. But he rejected both those theories as he progressed with his work. The real answer, Larry decided, lay in the pent-up power of his own unconscious.

While Larry had been climbing the ladder of success in his chosen field, he had actually envied writers like George, but had deliberately belittled their work rather than admit his own shortcomings. The proof of this lay in his eagerness to take on the historical assignment, which was a complete departure from the technical writing in which he was so adept. He wanted to show what he could do, but in order to do it his own way, he kept reverting to his usual style, keeping his conscious effort so fixed in its purpose that he completely rejected any unconscious urge to inject a real flair into his work. But he couldn't ignore the urge itself. His inner mind would not let him.

So Larry really knew before he was told that his history lacked something that only his old friend George could supply. In going through the material that George sent him, he realized that he had read it all before, but so passingly that he even forgot that Ambrose Winsted was mentioned. That was, he *consciously* forgot it, but unconsciously, he remembered it *in detail.* So when he dipped into the unconscious, it was only natural that the picture of Ambrose Winsted, the idol of his conscious mind, should fade into that of Gorge Sanville, his unconscious ideal, who bounced him right back to Ambrose Winsted as he really had been. The upshot was that Larry Burrick discovered his own unconscious potential and turned it to good advantage.

Sooner or later, nearly everyone is sure to have experiences comparable to the two just cited, although usually less intensely. My files contain hundreds of such cases. In many instances, people found themselves responding to their unconscious impressions and were able to straighten themselves out during the early stages of a dilemma. Others recalled that it had taken a series of such awakenings to get themselves on the right track. One might go into an introspective mood and eventually find the answer to some trifling problem. Another would become interested in a hobby, and by the time he got back to some project that had been worrying him, he would find that the situation had solved itself.

In such cases, the unconscious is working in installments, so to speak; the important factor here is that unconscious impressions can become so subtle that the people experiencing them may not even recognize their existence. I learned this by applying suggestion while questioning such people regarding their inner thoughts. When they laughed at the idea of unconscious impressions, I encouraged them to give examples showing how ridiculous such theories could be. The effort to recall what they regarded as trivial events invariably caused them to tap their own unconscious without realizing it, which in turn enabled me to probe their inner minds and offer further suggestions that would spur them to still more recollections.

If you depend entirely on your conscious mind as your absolute decision-maker, you are apt to resist or override the submerged impulses that assert themselves unconsciously; and the longer they are pent-up, the more forceful the jolt will be. At the other extreme, overdependence on the unconscious can result in wishful thinking that curbs the conscious mind. Making plans that you never put into practice can be just as devastating as running yourself ragged in the wrong direction. Either way, the awakening can be rude, and even though it may provide a real understanding of an individual's full potential, much valuable time may be wasted while waiting for results.

That is why my slogan is "The sooner the better" when I advise people how to coordinate their conscious life with their unconscious. The primary requirement is to make such coordination an integral part of your daily living, rather than wait for some problem to develop. In fact, a day-by-day or week-by-week procedure can often avert a crisis. By programming yourself along proven lines, you will know which of two alternatives to use when coping with changing circumstances. One is to follow the inclinations of your conscious mind, particularly in practical matters, while pausing at specified intervals to reflect on the wisdom of your choice.

This brings your unconscious to the fore, as though asking its approval. The other, which applies to more unusual circumstances, should be decided by the unconscious with the proviso that it meet whatever requirements the conscious mind may have.

The choice of these alternatives also depends on individual needs, as will be seen from cases cited in the following chapters; but they will all stress the importance of watching for the little things in life. What may seem a trifling coincidence may eventually loom much larger than something that appears more spectacular, yet does not change the over-all pattern of a person's life. Similarly, a passing fancy may carry great weight if you pause long enough to allow it headway, whereas something that seems momentous may rapidly dwindle if you depend on it too heavily. The more you follow the prescribed exercises, the better qualified you will become to team the conscious and the unconscious and get the most out of both.

I have found two factors so potent in such programming that each deserves a chapter in itself. One is the development of visual imagery through special exercises designed for that purpose. Used regularly, they will sharpen that latent faculty to such extent that instead of groping for impressions you will develop them automatically—even setting the pace for unconscious action rather than depending upon it. Some people who have utilized this process have described it as opening an inner world of the mind, with vistas all its own. My hope is that others will share that experience.

The other factor is the faculty of time projection, joining the past to the future with the present as the link. This is something that must be tried to be appreciated. Its chapter therefore contains many diverse examples of how it works, since each incident represents a highly personalized account that may strike home to each reader.

□ HOW TO RECALL "FORGOTTEN" EXPERIENCES OR □
LOCATE MISPLACED ITEMS

It has become more and more evident to me that trance states are self-delusionary and quite unnecessary in order to tap your inner mind. We find in examining so-called "hypnotic" age regression that subjects aren't actually reliving earlier life experiences as much as they are doing an excellent job of role playing and acting. It seems true, however, that such subjects are indeed able to recall details of earlier experiences. The key, of course, is not a hypnotic trance or some TM or alpha state but strong motivation and imagination.

The exercise I am going to explain is included in almost every lecture I give around the world; I do this as a mass test, with my entire theatre audience, and often with my television studio audiences in warming up their concentration before a program.

With eyes closed, picture either the sky or the sea. If you picture the sky, it is not enough that you picture a blue background (not everyone pictures scenes with color; not everyone necessarily dreams in color, although most people are unaware whether they do or do not dream in color). But, a blue background could simply be a bowl of ink and even if you can't get a blue background, it is important that you symbolize the meaningfulness of sky, by putting something in the sky that gives it the impression of sky—a cloud. If you are not getting color, such as white and blue, just put the shape of a cloud in the background of the sky. Try adding to this; if you are able to picture motion, fine—put a bird in the sky, or a plane, which, as you practice, you may almost be able to hear.

Now, if you are picturing the sea, all well and good, but it is not enough to picture just what seems like a blandness of blue or dark green; again, it could be a bowl of jello; you should put waves on the sea, and even try to add caps and motion to the waves.

If you are seeing the sky, you may hear wind, or a plane jetting through the sky. That's fine; the sound needn't be disturbing; it can be in the background; or the whistling of the wind, for instance, can be immensely restful.

If you picture waves and caps on the waves, then picture the turbulence of the sea, or make your image very restful by picturing the sea at the shore, and continue to hear the endless, rhythmic, churning of the waves.

I have gotten many reports of people who have found that this exercise has actually brought back forgotten memories. Go back in time in your life, trying to move back slowly, not in hours or minutes but in seconds, as if you were slowly floating back through the years, and pick up a scene in your life which perhaps you haven't thought about for a long, long time.

Try to imagine this scene as clearly as you can. If you can add color to the scene, fine. You should try to picture all the components of the scene, and it may take awhile, like a painter outlining a canvas to which you are later going to add color. As you picture the scene, you may also add motion; it is very possible through the various imagery exercises you have learned to add motion. Hold that scene in your mind for a minute or so, not much longer. Then, as you are holding the scene, find an object in the scene—it may be an object you haven't thought about in a long time.

If you are picturing a birthday party when you were seven years old, perhaps the door or the doorknob behind the kitchen table seems unimportant but, suddenly, you realize that it is there and you are picturing it. Hold onto the scene; hold onto the object; take three deep breaths and then, when you have exhaled the third breath, remove everything from the scene except the object—the doorknob, or the car, or the diving board—holding onto that for maybe ten seconds more. As you are doing that, you may suddenly start to recall other factors in the scene which you hadn't thought of before; the people who were there or other items in the scene may suddenly pop in and out. When you have done this for about ten seconds, or until there seems to be no further churning of memories in the scene, just forget about it, but *remember* the object. Within an hour after the experience, whether you are sitting in a movie theatre, reading the newspaper, or sitting in a bus, close your eyes again and picture only the object. You will find that, in a matter of seconds, the entire scene will flash back into your mind—usually more clearly than the first time; and in flashing back, further details will appear in your mind. You should end the scene, when it is fully developed, with the object, just the object, in your mind, forgetting about the rest of the scene, holding that for a few seconds.

The entire recall exercise should also be done before falling asleep at night. Write the object on a piece of paper and leave it by your bedside during the night. The next morning, when you get up, if you close your eyes and picture the scene, it will not only come back, but will be even more detailed. By using this as a recurring exercise, you can very possibly, in a short amount of time, reconstruct an experience in more detail than you have recalled in many years. This is similar to the techniques I used when I was called in by the Reno Police Department in early 1977, regarding the clarification of witnesses' memories of a suspect in the murder of a University of Nevada coed. By the time I had finished with the four witnesses, each of whom felt that they had seen no one that clearly, three were so vivid in their recall that they each described the suspect in exactly the same details, although they had only glanced over towards the suspect out of the car in which they were riding, and which was moving so rapidly that they had only given a casual glance at what turned out to be the key suspect.

In locating "lost" or what are really misplaced objects, naturally there must be some memory of your last contact with it. You should try to recall this scene. When you wipe away the scene, picture only the "lost" item for ten seconds. Before falling asleep, write the item on a piece of paper and leave it by your bedside. Practice again on awakening in the morning.

□ 3 □

UNLOCKING THE
SECRETS OF THE
INNER MIND

Concentration and mental imagery are two natural functions of the human mind that tap the unconscious.

You don't need chants or spells to raise your unconscious mind to the working level. All you need is practice in translating outer observations to inner impressions, so that they can be returned with interest as guidelines for conscious action. In the preceding chapter I showed how this can occur spontaneously; now I shall explain how you can stimulate and even trigger such action through your own effort, thus turning it into a two-way procedure.

In earlier exercises you learned to concentrate first through the simple count, then by the reverse count. This enabled you to focus your mind on visual imagery involving melting processes and color blending. These techniques cleared your conscious mind of outer impressions, enabling your unconscious to thrust its inner impressions to the fore. But those can be feeble or difficult to classify unless translated into outer terms. So as a preliminary stimulus toward unconscious expression, the following exercise is both logical and practical.

Instead of concentrating upon a mind-clearing process, focus your thoughts on a "mind objective." That may sound like an odd term, but I have chosen it for that very reason; that you have an object in mind that you can appreciate both outwardly and inwardly.

Begin with this: What do you like best?

Suppose it's bowling. You picture yourself bowling a ball down the alley, until—wham!—it hits the pins and knocks them for a strike. You not only see it; you hear it.

Suppose it's dancing. You picture yourself in the arms of the one that you love, with the music that you both like best. You not only see it; you not only hear it; you feel it.

Suppose it's anything else. From there on, it's your ticket. Just think of whatever you would like most and your inner self will reflect it.

There is no need to break down the process at this stage; we are dealing with a preliminary exercise that will vary with individuals. Moreover, the results will probably be fragmentary or irregular and may be lacking in visual imagery almost entirely. Ideas, impressions, recollections may furnish visual suggestions along with other sensory reactions. The purpose is to build these to the point where they can be fully identified and used to create further and stronger images. That can be accomplished through the exercises that follow.

□ STRETCHING THE IMAGINATION □

Here you can prove to your own satisfaction that there are times when you can see certain things better with your eyes shut. The method is to study a simple object and give your imagination sufficient leeway to picture it as something more complex. Then, by merely closing your eyes, you can shake off the shackles of reality and transform the actual object into the visual form of what you think it ought to be. To stimulate the process, you use a simple diagram consisting of two concentric circles, as shown here; then begin with the first exercise as described:

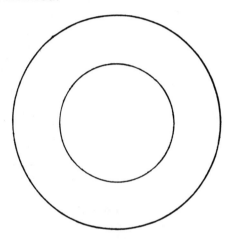

FIRST EXERCISE: EXPANDED MOTION

Step One: Study the diagram and keep thinking how the two circles resemble an automobile tire. Once you have that fixed in mind, continue with:

Step Two : Think of the tire being mounted on the rear wheel of an automobile. Follow that with:

Step Three: Thoughts of the tire beginning to spin, wheel and all, slowly at first; then more rapidly.

Step Four: During that action, let your mental imagery expand to include the entire car, rolling along a highway.

Step Five: Review those steps and list them mentally in order: Tire—Wheel—Spin—Car.

Step Six: Close your eyes and visualize the steps you have imagined, carrying your picturization as far beyond the listed limits as it wants to go.

In each of the exercises given, you can vary the steps to suit your own inclinations. The tire, for instance, could be rolling down the street like a large hoop; or the tube could widen as you enter it, so you could find yourself in a fabulous cavern before reaching the outlet. But instead of using the same initial concept to repeat the exercise, it is preferable to picture the two circles as representing something completely different as a starter, with each inspiring its own series of thought trains. Here is a list:

Automobile tire	Wishing well	Knob on a safe
Elongated tube	(from above)	Holly wreath
Small coin on large coin	Bull's-eye target	Cup and saucer
Doughnut	Quoit	Dinner plate
Life preserver	Telephone dial	Gun muzzle
Metal washer	Soup bowl	End of water pipe
Candy mint	Round mirror	Bowl of smoking pipe
Hat (from above)	Ship's porthole	Ashtray
Picture frame	End of a pencil	Telephone mouthpiece
Large button	Fried egg	Roll of paper
Officer's badge	Doorbell	Typewriter key

SUMMARY OF FIRST EXERCISE: Basically, there is no need to go beyond the specified limits as the purpose of the exercise is to train your mind's "eye" in picking up details. If the spinning tire rolls right out of your mental picture, it will have served its purpose and you can go on to another exercise. But if it rouses your interest in the car, where it is going, the people who are in it, or whatever else may develop, it is a good plan to pursue it further.

SECOND EXERCISE: PERSPECTIVE

Step One: Using the same diagram, think of the two circles as a tube viewed from one end, represented by the larger circle.

Step Two: To aid that concept, close your eyes briefly after Step 1, to get the effect of elongation.

Step Three: Open your eyes; then close them and expand the tube in size, so that it forms a darkened tunnel with a tiny exit at the far end.

Step Four: Imagine yourself entering the tunnel at a rapid speed, with the far end growing larger and larger as you approach it.

Step Five: Suddenly, you burst out of the far end of the tunnel into broad daylight.

SUMMARY OF SECOND EXERCISE: Again you have fulfilled the purpose of the exercise, with your personal involvement adding an advanced form of mental imagery. If further impressions develop as a result, stay with them and see where they lead.

Some of these imaginary objects should be embellished a trifle to start. Give a target a few more circles with the center as a bull's-eye. With a telephone dial, the space between the inner and outer circles would need round holes to represent the numbers. A typewriter key should have a letter to identify it; and so on. Other ideas will suggest themselves to you automatically as you proceed.

Go beyond mere visualization in as many steps as possible. With a doughnut, sensations of touch and taste could occur immediately. Picking up coins, you could hear the clink and sense the weight. Pressing a doorbell involves touch followed by an auditory impression of a ringing sound. Smoke coming from a pipe or ashtray could suggest the smell of tobacco. Applying these sensory concepts to the improvement of visual imagery will prove a great asset toward total mind control.

SHIFTING SCENES

The exercises just detailed clearly show how you can start with one simple object and form a chain of others, link by link. But the question remains: Where does the chain end? The answer is—Nowhere, unless you can build a simple diagram into a full-fledged picture that becomes a basis for more of the same. All along you may have glimmerings of this, but they may simply drift into ideas instead of mental concepts with a solid, substantial form.

Here is an exercise whereby your mind's eye can actually duplicate an effect of physical vision, thus serving as a basis for further advanced tests. By following the exercise closely, you will gain the knack of "shifting scenes" after forming a solid picture that may become top-heavy and break the chain through its own weight. Once you know that you can not only keep a three-dimensional image in mind, but also change it while envisioning it, you can go on to bigger things.

The device used is the diagram shown here:

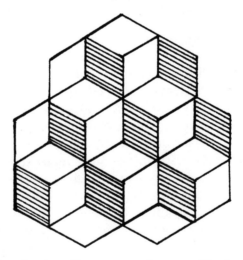

Step One: Study the diagram and you will observe that it apparently consists of six cubes in an upright stack, giving a *three-dimensional* effect.

Step Two: Keep watching the cubes and suddenly the *six* will become *seven,* when viewing the cubes from below instead of from above.

Step Three: Repeat the experiment, keeping your eyes focused on the top of the stack. Count the seconds, using the Second Count (page 6) until the cubes again change from six to seven, while their perspective also changes.

Step Four: Do the same with the reverse change from seven cubes to six, again counting the seconds as you do. Again, finish the count when the change is complete.

NOTE: Steps 3 and 4 should be repeated several times in order to adjust your timing. The purpose of the Second Count is not to acquire speed but to gain consistency. If you find that a change is delayed too long, a slight change of your gaze will speed the process. Check this with the next two steps:

Step Five: To fix the cubes at six, focus your gaze on the top front corner of the uppermost cube in the stack of six. This will emphasize the three top cubes of the "six stack," although you will be *aware* of the bottom row of three that forms the base of the stack.

Step Six: Relax your gaze and focus on the lower front corner of the top cube. This slight shift should bring an immediate change from six cubes to seven. This will emphasize two inverted cubes side by side, with a single inverted cube just below them. But you will be *aware* of two cubes flanking the single, and two cubes side by side below that.

After repeating Steps 5 and 6 a few times, pause and review what you have done. In a definite sense, you have caused objects to change in number at regular intervals through applied concentration. Now you are ready to continue the process through your own power of visual imagery, for more important than the change in number is the fact that you have caused the cubes to *alter their perspective,* which becomes your real goal in the steps that follow:

Step Seven: Study the diagram below and you will see exactly what the three uppermost cubes looked like when you focused your gaze on the stack of six, as described in Step 5. Here the bottom row has been eliminated, because although you were aware of that row your gaze was focused on these three.

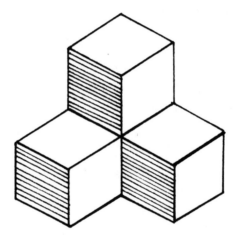

Step Eight: Read this step through before proceeding. After studying the three cubes, close your eyes and visualize them just as you have seen them. Think of the stack as being slightly below your eye level, so that it will seem that you are looking downward at the cubes. Once you have this image fixed in mind, open your eyes.

Step Nine: Now study the diagram on page 43 and you will see how the three uppermost cubes appeared when you fixed your gaze on the group of seven. Again, the bottom row has been eliminated to emphasize the three at the top. Get these well focused as you did before.

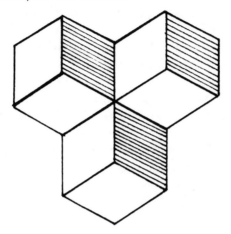

Step Ten: Again, read through the step before you proceed. Close your eyes and visualize the three cubes exactly as you have seen them here. Picture the cubes above your eye level, so you will be seeing the bottom of the single cube beneath the other two. After fixing the image, open your eyes.

NOTE: Keep concentrating on the three cubes as described and it won't matter if you picture any additional cubes from the group of seven (as in Step 6.)

Now read the next two steps carefully in detail before proceeding with them, as your eyes will be closed throughout the entire procedure:

Step Eleven: Close your eyes and visualize three cubes as viewed from above (Step 9). After your mental gaze is fully focused on that image, let your gaze work slowly downward, forming the entire stack of six (Step 1). Focus your mental gaze on the bottom row of the stack. Hold it there briefly; then let it relax.

Step Twelve: As you relax your mental gaze, picture the lower cubes inverting themselves, so that you seem to view them from below. Work your gaze upward, forming the inverted group of seven cubes (Step 2). As you reach the top, concentrate on a single cube with two above it, all inverted. (Step 10). Hold that briefly, then relax.

Step Thirteen: Now picture your gaze going just a trifle higher, so that you can look down on the upper surface of a single cube. Almost instantly, the inverted image will be gone and you will find yourself back at your starting point, viewing three standard cubes from above (Step 9). Open your eyes to complete the exercise.

REPEATING THE PROCEDURE

You are now set to repeat the final procedure by simply closing your eyes and letting your mental gaze work downward to the bottom of the stack; then upward to the top; down again, up again, as often as desired. By using a slow count, you can hold each completed image for a specified period before encouraging another change from six cubes to seven or vice versa.

During early training, you will find that eye motion helps, even though you keep your eyes closed through a series of changes . This is because you are simulating the action that you underwent while actually studying the diagrams. Gradually, this can be reduced until you reach a balance point where you will be depending almost entirely on visualization, with no up-and-down motion to force a change of perspective. When the upright stack begins to melt into the inverted group, you should find yourself focusing directly on the three sets (as depicted under Steps 7 and 9).

As an ultimate goal, you can concentrate on a single cube rather than three, letting it shape itself in upright form, line by line. By having it shift upward, bringing the bottom into view, you can picture new lines forming beneath as those representing the top are obscured from view. This is visual imagery at its best, as you not only are fixing upon an idea—you are causing it to shift to another concept. Once acquired, this ability can be applied to more elaborate forms of picturization.

DEVELOPING IMPRESSIONS

Here is another optical experiment that can be turned into an effective exercise in visual imagery. Basically, it consists of changing a "negative" into a "positive" impression (much like the development of a photographic plate), which can be followed by retention of the impression thus gained, which in turn is subject to later recall.

Step One: Read the accompanying instructions carefully so that you can follow them step by step without interruption, as timing is important in this exercise.

Step Two: Have a strong light available as well as a white or light-colored surface like a wall, curtain, screen, or large sheet of paper.

Step Three: Gaze intently at the "negative" portrait shown on page 46, focusing directly on the white spot in the center.

Step Four: Count off thirty seconds, using the Mental Time Count (page 6) while keeping your gaze fixed on the spot.

Step Five: Now look at the white surface, keeping your eyes steadily on one area and a "positive" or reverse image will develop in full form.

Step Six: As you watch, the picture will fade, only to reappear again. By blinking your eyes a few times, you can speed this process.

NOTE: What you have done here is create an afterimage that to your eyes *seems* real and therefore has an existence *in your mind*. The "negative" on which you focused *was* real, and from it you created a "positive" you saw as clearly as the "negative"—perhaps more clearly, because the switch from one phase to the other tends to improve the impression. So much for the optical effect. Now, through further steps, you can transfer the creative process to a phase of visual imagery:

Step Seven: Closing your eyes, concentrate on the positive impression you have gained and hold it in mind for a count of ten to fifteen seconds.

Step Eight: Open your eyes, then close them again and visualize the mental picture more in detail, holding it for a longer count—perhaps twenty seconds.

Steps Nine and Ten: These are simply a repetition of Steps 7 and 8, done at intervals of a few minutes in order to test your ability at *retention* as well as improving the picture. Here, your mind's eye takes over in full.

ADDING THE ELEMENT OF RECALL

After you have fully familiarized yourself with the exercise of Developing Impressions, you can repeat in detail the last four steps (7 through 10) a few hours later, or even the next day. This will be an exercise in recall as a contrast to simple retention. If the image develops clearly and easily, well and good; you can try it at further intervals on the same basis. Any time you fail to recognize the positive picture clearly or find that you have to strain to recall it, you can resort to a refresher by referring back to the original "negative" and going through the entire exercise just as you did originally (Steps 1 through 10).

This repetition of the original exercise can serve a two-fold purpose: (1) Each time you go through the whole procedure, it should develop more rapidly than before; and (2) The positive impression should become sharper and more familiar. Combined, these factors show that your ability at developing visual imagery is improving and thereby becoming a natural adjunct of your inner mind, symbolizing the creative process. Any improvement gained through such repetition is of the utmost importance.

SIMPLIFIED PICTURIZATION

This is really an important form of portrait picturization, requiring no special preparation and thereby serving as a preliminary to the more advanced procedures. All you need is a small portrait of a person—for convenience you can use the picture of Washington that appears on the United States dollar bill.

Step One: Study Washington's portrait on the bill casually for ten or fifteen seconds; since you are already familiar with it, this is practically automatic. Then read the next step.

Step Two: Close your eyes and visualize the portrait, giving special attention to any details you may have missed, specifically: (a) the direction of his gaze, (b) the expression of his lips, (c) the size of his ears. Then open your eyes.

Step Three: Compare your visualization with the actual portrait you viewed. Check Washington's features, particularly those specified as *a, b,* and *c.*

Step Four: Now close your eyes again and visualize the portrait with all those points corrected. If already correct, simply emphasize them.

Step Five: After opening your eyes, study the portrait to see if (a) your visualization was entirely correct and (b) if so, how much sharper the portrait now appears to you.

Step Six: Close your eyes and "see" the portrait as it now appears. Try to add realism to your mental picture along with mobility of expression, such as having the eyes change direction or the lips show new expression. Open your eyes to conclude the exercise.

The same procedure can be applied to bills of various denominations: Washington, $1; Jefferson, $2; Lincoln, $5; Hamilton, $10; Jackson, $20; Grant, $50; Franklin, $100. As well as animating your own visualization, it is a good test to try on friends, letting them look at a portrait on a bill and then look away while you query them regarding it. Washington's ears make a good catch question, because his wig hides them in the portrait. In fact, only Lincoln and Grant have ears that show conspicuously, if at all. Jackson's gaze is also worthy of close study, because for a while it was used as the principal way of detecting counterfeit $20 notes. The forger who engraved the illegal plates made Jackson noticeably cross-eyed.

ADVANCED PICTURIZATION

Rather than carry Simplified Picturization beyond the limited stage just described, it is better to move right into an advanced procedure. Here you need a good photograph for a start; if several are available, so much the better. Pictures of a friend or a person you expect to meet are highly recommended.

Step One: Study the photo in over-all form. As a full face, it can be classified as: (a) *oval,* which is rounded, but also somewhat elongated; (b) *square,* which has the same width at the temples as at the jaws, and (c) *triangular,* wide at the top and narrow at the bottom. All three shapes are shown here:

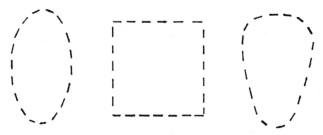

Step Two: Now fill in the features—eyes, nose, and mouth. Close your own eyes and visualize them as you saw them. From there, develop them through:

Step Three: Filling in the details—eyebrows, hairlines, ears, perhaps mustaches and beards or exotic hairdos.

Step Four: Refer back to the original photo and decide how far you have developed it. Or, if you meet the person whose photo you have studied, check your accuracy.

NOTE: This exercise can be repeated at intervals, using the same person's photo or switching to another if you prefer. Either way, you can follow up with the more advanced:

AUDIO-VISUAL SYSTEM

In this exercise no photo is needed, though one can be used for reference if available. You must, however, be fairly well acquainted with the person or persons you have decided to concentrate upon during this test.

Step One: Form a mental image of your subject and *immediately* give it mobility, such as change of gaze and expression. Read through the instructions; then keep your eyes lightly shut during the succeeding steps.

Step Two: Picture the person speaking, either to you or to someone else or both. This will allow turns of the person's head from full face or profile. Keep focusing on the person's lip movements.

Step Three: Try to catch what the person is saying—not just visually, but audibly as well. Any movement will naturally be visible, but try to gain a sound effect to go with it. Any tone or greeting characteristic of the person will serve as a link to:

Step Four: Here, you tune into snatches of conversation, directed to you or to somebody else. Let words carry the impression, particularly their inflection or emphasis, with changes of expression simply an accompaniment. From this stage, you merge into:

Step Five: This involves the person in a direct discussion, the telling of an anecdote, or some other characteristic phase with which you are familiar. Try to balance sight with sound to the point where each emphasizes the other.

Step Six: Conclude your "interview" by opening your eyes and reflecting on what took place. Then, half-closing your eyes, try to fill in little details you might have noted, with anything from jests to gestures serving as both vocal and visual aids.

NOTE: Repetition of this exercise can often bring results that are amazing. You will find that you begin to know your friends better through visual imagery than in real life. When you meet a person with whom you have had these mental get-togethers, you can actually pick up from where you left off imaginatively, thus adding more impact.

☐ TELEPHONIC INTERLUDE ☐

If the subject you choose for a series of audio-visual exercises is readily available, you can telephone him or her between tests and discuss subjects that came to your mind during the imaginary interview. Here, instead of proceeding with new steps, you concentrate on one thing only. While you talk and let your subject open new channels of thought along with those you suggest, keep visualizing the person, keeping your eyes closed, or turning out a light so that you are in a darkened corner, or even an obscure phone booth.

This will enable you to utilize actual audio to induce video projections, a remarkable combination. Ordinarily, your mental imagery must be controlled to keep it from outrunning the auditory effects you are seeking to induce. But here, with conversation taking the lead, you can give your mind's eye unrestricted range. For an over-all sequence, try a series of step-by-step exercises as described; inject a few telephonic interludes among them; and finish with an actual get-together with your subject.

TELEVISION EXERCISES

NOTE: As a special exercise in developing both visual and auditory imagery, select a TV personality as your subject, particularly a person who appears frequently, such as a newscaster or someone regularly reporting on sports or weather. Study that person's speech and actions; then, between shows, use mental imagery to test your recall.

□ 4 □
PUTTING THE INNER MIND TO WORK

In the days of the one-room country school house, knowledge was measured in terms of the "Three Rs"—Reading, 'Riting, and 'Rithmetic. These still serve as symbols of the outer mind. Highly technical studies tend to develop a slide-rule mentality, just as a singsong alphabet or reciting "Two times two are four" became a matter of rote in the old days. The only difference was that back then, when a grammar-school diploma was less common than a college degree today, people could spend a lot more time following their own intuition than studying a vast variety of subjects.

There are exceptions, of course, such as the modern field of parapsychology, with its emphasis on such phenomena as peak clairvoyancy and telepathy. Formerly, such things were regarded as superstitions or delusions: Today, they are deemed worthy of scientific survey except by die-hard doubters. But even the proponents of parapsychology have buried themselves in a maze of statistics and heaps of paperwork, trying to prove mathematically something that they already accept as established fact.

Somewhere between these two extremes lies an area in

which the elements of both can be happily blended; the Three Rs of the inner mind, which can be listed in the following order:

Recognition: The establishment and absorption of a fixed fact into one's thinking.
Retention: The filing of such facts for later reference.
Realization and *Recall:* The recall and application of such facts to some purpose.

These three phases can be identified as *Past, Present,* and *Future.* With the old Three Rs the idea was to keep them continually present. By reciting the letters of the alphabet, schoolchildren learned to form words that were used in contests called spelling bees. Having mastered the multiplication tables during arithmetic class, they were ready for the binomial theorem when they reached algebra. Each new item was added to the stockpile. With Reading, 'Riting, 'Rithmetic and their offshoots, this was done through a fourth R called Rote, whereby the outer mind crammed home its facts and kept repeating them to the point where they were fixed, hopefully for all time.

With the modern Three Rs, any number of facts can be stored away without the aid of rote except in occasional instances where it serves as a booster. Many can be registered instantly, because they are recognized as important. From that fixed point of Recognition, representing the past, you can mentally picture a continuous line, standing for Retention, as the ever-changing present. At the far end, you have the third R, Realization, its exact position not yet determined because it signifies some future time when you may need to use that fact for some special purpose. Yet almost anywhere along the line in between, you can tap that reservoir of Retention through a fourth R, *Recall.*

How can you obtain this ability to probe your inner mind? By dropping the narrow policy of doing the same thing over and over. Broaden your activity and increase its range. Make it a habit to weigh ideas, even noting trivial things you might ordinarily overlook. It is as easy as learning your ABCs by rote; indeed easier, for recall becomes spontaneous, the more you develop it. You don't have to become tired as your conscious mind pounds the same thing over and over into your unconscious.

Instead, you let your conscious mind implant the germ of an idea in your unconscious, so that it can grow there. In short, you give a second thought to things—the first consciously, the second unconsciously. Later, it will tend to bounce back in the form of instant recall; this interchange between the conscious and the unconscious (or vice versa) may continue at intervals, according to the importance of the item involved. The idea may also be brought to the conscious mind when you encounter some new fact related to the one that you unconsciously stored away. This may have a special significance, particularly if it occurs repeatedly or in some striking fashion, much like the ringing of a telephone bell that captures your attention.

Through concentration, visual imagery, and their exercises you have already learned to tap the hidden resources of the unconscious. Thus, in using those techniques, you are automatically taking advantage of ideas that have been filed in the inner mind. The next step is to study and analyze case histories where the unconscious has asserted itself through the conscious mind, even producing the equivalent of physical or sensory reactions. From these instances you will learn what to look for in similar experiences of your own: How to separate the meaningful from the meaningless; how to interpret the various results; how to identify the motivations that are apt to produce the strongest and most important results.

As a first example, I shall describe one of my own personal experiences in inner-mind expansion that shows how suddenly and surprisingly these things can happen. During my early days as an entertainer, I put on magic shows for Scout troops, civic clubs, schools, and other groups. As I improved my skills and expanded my repertoire, I began booking myself into various small-town auditoriums, including firehouses that had an upstairs hall. That meant meeting people, remembering them for future reference, and making contacts all along the line. Of course, I listed the names of good contacts, but often it was just a matter of remembering someone whose name would probably spring to mind if needed.

During those formative years, I delved into mentalism and soon turned my thoughts to ESP, or extra-sensory perception. I found that results in this field depended on mind conditioning, so I applied it to every phase of my work. If I happened to be booked for a fire-hall show, I wouldn't say to myself, "This is just another of those routine jobs." I would say, "This is going to be the best fire-hall show anyone ever saw." I reasoned it this way: Most fire-hall shows were disappointing, because nobody was organized. The acts came in and expected everything to run smoothly, as it would in a theater. But always something was sure to bog down: curtains, scenery, dressing rooms, acoustics, footlights, floodlights—you name it! Everybody would always blame everybody else after the fiasco was over.

To avoid that, I would not only plan my show in detail a day or so before, I would also go through all the stage preparations just as if I were at the hall itself. No rehearsal, real or imaginary, can be of any use if stage directions go wrong at a crucial moment. So here I was, back home, picturing myself on the stage of a fire hall in the little town of Hilldale, where I had never been before, calling for "Lights" that seemed to come on with an actual glare before my tightly closed eyes. I must have worked my mental imagery up to a fever pitch, for I suddenly heard a voice calling, "Mr. Kreskin! Wait! I want to talk to you! Wait!"

As my eyes popped open, I seemed momentarily blinded by the glare; then I realized that I was home, but with the echo of that voice—a woman's voice—still ringing in my ears: "Wait!" I'd had realistic mental projections before, but never any as vivid as that, for it really left me shaken, wondering if something was due to happen in Hilldale that might prevent me from going there, or which—even worse—could mean trouble if I did go. All the next day, while I was rehearsing or packing apparatus, my mind would flash back to that voice. Rather than interpret its inflection as a warning, I felt that I might be neglecting something in regard to Hilldale, so I double-checked all my props, my time schedule, and even the correspondence confirming the exact date of the show.

My qualms came back when I reached Hilldale, for the fire hall seemed oddly familiar. I shrugged that off by deciding that almost every fire hall looked like any other fire hall, and I had played a lot of them. I set up my show without a hitch, found that the stage was well equipped and the crew so competent that a detailed checkup seemed unnecessary. That was why I insisted on one, for I realized by then that it was about the only thing that could possibly be neglected. It took longer than I had expected and when I came to the final item, the testing of the spotlight, I suddenly felt shaky, for this was the crux of the whole thing. I was about to turn my mental imagery into actuality.

I felt that maybe the spotlight wouldn't work; or if it did, it would either blow a fuse or cause a short circuit. I was keyed for anything except what really happened. As I waved my arms, calling for the spot, it came on perfectly and there I was, master of the stage, ready for the show to come, bathed in a glory of brilliance that wiped out my qualms completely. So I stood there, enjoying it, about to spread my arms and say "Turn it off!" when out of the blackness beyond that brilliance came a voice that said: "Mr. Kreskin! Wait! I want to talk to you! Wait!"

It was uncanny. The thing I had imagined was being

reenacted in reality. I tried to find where the voice came from, but I was so blinded by the light that I couldn't see anything in the blackness beyond. Before I had been able to blink my eyes and get rid of the whole scene; now I was trapped in the midst of it. Finally, out of the blackness a happy, friendly, middle-aged lady emerged. In the glare of the spotlight, she clasped her hands over mine and told me: "I'm Edith Lorman—Tom Lorman's mother. He said you would be coming this way someday and he has been so anxious for me to meet you—"

The name Tom Lorman not only broke the spell, it filled in all the details that I needed, invoking memories that clarified the whole situation. Tom was a close friend whom I hadn't seen since around the time I had started performing in fire halls and he had told me back then that his father had been the fire chief in a small town called Hilldale and if I ever played the place, he wanted me to make it a point to look up his family and introduce myself. I recalled jotting down the name at the time, but I had lost my memo and I didn't think it mattered, because I expected to be seeing Tom again. Instead, I hadn't and during the interim I had lost all track of him. It wasn't until I was getting ready for the Hilldale show that the name of the town, plus the fact that I was actually going there, triggered an unconscious reaction that I partly identified but failed to amplify. That's often the way when unconscious impressions come to the surface. Being a form of suggestion, they are apt to be misinterpreted by the conscious mind, which means that you will have to probe for the right answer, unless some other unconscious impulse provides an added clue.

Many students of parapsychology would be inclined to attribute this case to precognition, due to the fact that Tom's mother voiced the very words that I heard mentally more than twenty-four hours earlier under almost identical circumstances, while others may feel that telepathy played a strong part. While not rejecting either of those theories, I can still see how the long arm of coincidence may have been involved. After the show, I met Tom's family and learned that in writing to them at intervals, he always asked if they had heard from me. As a result, Tom's mother had kept me increasingly in mind and when she learned that at last I was due to appear at the local fire hall, she was naturally eager to welcome me at the first opportunity, in case I had forgotten my promise to Tom or had been reticent about contacting his family at that late date.

Being familiar with the fire hall, Mrs. Lorman had come there while we were setting the stage, but had waited until the last minute; then, realizing that I was about to leave, she had hurried forward, calling for me to wait. Since I hadn't noticed her until I heard her voice, the sudden flashback to the very thing I was anticipating naturally astounded me and may even have caused me to exaggerate the similarity between the two calls. At the same time, it should be noted how closely this conformed to the Three Rs of the inner mind. I had *recognized* Tom's request in the past, *retained* it during an ever-changing present, and finally *realized* it at the Hilldale fire hall. But it was largely that fourth R, representing Recall, that brought my inner mind into focus on the imagery that was to become reality.

In contrast to the case that I have cited, partly because it is still so vivid in my mind, there are countless others that are found in everyday living and therefore should be cultivated to the full. This is where you can gain results so quickly and spontaneously that you are apt to take them for granted unless you analyze them sufficiently to note what really happened. Here is a case that sets the pattern.

Irma Gladney and her husband Roy were great football fans, so they bought four tickets for the big game to be played at State Stadium, a few hours' drive away—two for themselves and two for their friends the Crofts, who lived in another town. The tickets were delivered at the Gladney home a few days before the game and with each pair was a special permit for a parking area. Holders of a permit could park inside the area and wait until friends arrived and spotted their car, so it didn't really matter who arrived first, as it would work either way.

Since time was short until the big day, Irma and Roy decided not to mail the two tickets to the Crofts. So Irma telephoned them long distance and explained the situation, saying: "We don't want to take a risk with the tickets as they'll be no good to anybody if they are delayed in the mail. So instead, we're just sending you a permit that will admit you to the special parking area and whichever of us gets there first can wait for the others to show up. Okay?"

It was okay with the Crofts, so Irma suggested that they bring sandwiches and hot coffee; then Roy took the phone and added that they would all walk from the parking area to the stadium together. So with everything nicely arranged, Roy Gladney mailed the parking permit to George Croft and everybody was happy—except Irma. She began to worry; since the tickets were safely tucked away, she decided that maybe their car wasn't in shape for the trip. Roy had it checked, and all proved fine. Still, Irma worried; now it had to be the weather, but the big day dawned perfect. So Irma decided to relax and forget her silly qualms. Being somewhat familiar with visual imagery, she applied the countdown system with the melting process and it worked like a charm.

Irma pictured herself at the stadium so clearly that she fancied she heard the cheers of the crowd as the game was about to start. She turned to Roy who was beside her, but he was so engrossed that she turned the other way to tell the Crofts how glad she was. All Irma saw was a pair of empty seats, the only ones vacant in that sea of spectators! Aghast, Irma bounded out to the kitchenette where Roy was making coffee and moments later she was telling him: "Roy! Something must have happened to the Crofts! They aren't going to be at the game. Call them right away and find out what's happened!"

While Roy made the call, Irma told him about her vivid impression of the empty seats and a few minutes later, Roy was laughingly repeating it to George Croft, who answered from the other end that everything was all right there. Still, Irma couldn't shake off that image of the empty seats. Snatching the phone from Roy, Irma demanded: "George! Did you get that letter—the one Roy mailed—"

"Not yet," interposed George, "but it's sure to be in our box at the post office. We're stopping there to pick up the mail on our way to the game and we're just leaving now."

"But maybe Roy made a mistake and put your stadium tickets in it. If the letter isn't there, you'll miss the game. It's sold out!"

By then, Roy was taking the phone from Irma, telling her not to get hysterical; next, he was reassuring George: "I have the tickets right here in my pocket, George. So don't worry if that letter isn't there. There's nothing in it but that parking permit, so you can park somewhere else if you don't get it. We'll meet you just as we planned—"

Hearing all that, Irma was grabbing the phone again, but now she was tense, decisive; not hysterical: "George, I see it now. If you don't get that permit, you can't meet us as planned, because they won't let you into the parking area. You will have to park somewhere else, as Roy says."

"That's right," came George's reply. "But where?"

"I'll tell you where." Irma turned to Roy. "Let me have those tickets, Roy. I'll read them off to George, so he will know where he and Doralene are going." Read them off Irma did, while George jotted them down: "Gate Two, Portal Nine—that's where we'll meet you, George, with your tickets. I'd better give you the rest, anyway. You'll be in Section

Twenty-seven, Row J—" There Irma paused, to add with a note of satisfaction: "Seats Seven and Eight."

Those were the very seats that Irma had pictured as empty, but that day they proved to be occupied, thanks to Irma's prevision of what didn't happen. The letter wasn't at the post office when the Crofts stopped there, so they left their car in a public parking lot and met Irma and Roy at Portal Nine. That's the great thing about visual imagery. It may invoke impressions of things that really happen, but it also can start a chain reaction that may turn everything the other way about as it did in this case.

What makes this case important is the fact that it represents hundreds—thousands—of examples that are going on every day. When analyzed, the answer sounds very simple, so obvious that you wonder why the people involved didn't figure it out in the first place. But the conscious mind doesn't work that way. It reads advertisements, billboards, slogans, catch phrases, whatever it picks up momentarily. It jumps to conclusions and builds improbabilities into impossibilities that finally crash because of their own weight, or drift merrily off into the great blue yonder just through the lack of balance. It takes the unconscious to come up with the real answers when they are really needed.

Probe your own unconscious and you will discover that it is waiting to be tapped in a fashion similar to the two cases I have just detailed. Both come under the head of "unfinished business." Everybody can recall someone they should have met or would like to meet. We all can think back to certain matters we regarded as nicely set and ready to go, yet which somehow left us a bit worried or uncertain because of a factor that was not apparent to our conscious thinking. So it pays to be constantly on the alert for such things. However, there is a third class of inner experiences: one where some pent-up hope or ambition not only is deeply stored away but may actually be supplanted by some other purpose that is seemingly vital but is really only a substitute.

The deeper a person delves into such a situation, the less it helps; the unconscious mind will resist because it has come to accept the dictum of the conscious. But catch it off guard, let something unexpected release the stifled power, and a whole career can be changed overnight. Many people have experienced this in modified form or in successive stages, but the most striking cases are those in which the result has been immediate, which is the reason I have chosen the following example.

Howard Thurston, America's leading magician over a period of nearly thirty years, first felt the spell of the mystic art as a boy of seven, when he witnessed the performance of Herrmann the Great in his home town of Columbus, Ohio. To young Howard, that was an evening of enchantment, but poverty and other problems banished any youthful dreams of becoming a magician in his own right. In his early teens, he became a jockey and when he grew too heavy to continue riding, he worked at the racetracks until finally the hope of leading a more useful life gave him the urge to become a medical missionary. He went to school in Massachusetts, where he occasionally entertained his fellow students with some makeshift magic tricks he had picked up here and there. After graduating at the age of twenty-two, Thurston started for Philadelphia to enroll in the University of Pennsylvania Medical School. While changing trains at Albany, he saw a lithograph of Herrmann the Great and decided to stay overnight and again see the show he had witnessed fifteen years before. What happened can best be told in Thurston's own words.

As I sat in the balcony I felt the thrills of enchantment that had captivated me in Columbus. I waited at the stage door and followed my idol to the hotel, just as I had done when a boy of seven in

Columbus, upon that other wonderful night. All night I fought desire and duty. Magician or medical missionary? Both offered adventure. My consuming desire was for magic, but duty won and when I entered the station the next morning I had reconciled myself to the work I had planned.

Suddenly Herrmann and Madame Herrmann appeared at the train gate. He was wearing a great fur coat and a slouch hat; a big diamond pin ornamented his shirt front and he carried a gold-headed cane. His mustache and goatee, the pulled-down slouch hat over his large, black eyes, gave him an almost satanic appearance. I heard the guard say to Herrmann:

"Syracuse—eight twenty."

Now comes the strangest part of the whole incident, which bears out what I have often said—that a man is not his own master in certain critical moments.

I went to the ticket window, laid down a twenty-dollar bill and asked for a ticket to Philadelphia. I placed the ticket in my pocket and counted the change.

"You've made a mistake," I said to the agent. "The price to Philadelphia is five dollars and twenty cents, but you have charged me only two dollars and eight cents."

He replied in a gruff voice: "You said Syracuse."

I looked at the ticket, then at Herrmann.

"All right," I said, "I'll go to Syracuse."

Thurston took the train to Syracuse and saw the Herrmann show on successive nights, imbibing every detail. From there, he continued to his father's home in Detroit, where he spent all his time practicing what magic he already knew and learning more until he was good enough to join a circus sideshow. It took him eight years to become a headliner in vaudeville and it was almost eight more before he had a big show of his own, but he stayed with it and during the next twenty-five years built it into the greatest and most profitable magic show of all time.

All those years Thurston continually attributed his success to the ticket-window incident, insisting that he had said "Philadelphia," not "Syracuse," so the ticketseller must have been wrong. But the inner mind has a way of speaking for itself, even to the point where a person's own autosuggestion causes him to say something he wants to say instead of what he really thinks he did say, without realizing it. There are also special cases—and I have personally checked out a surprising number of these—where someone is so intent upon an idea that another person has picked up the impression even though it was not expressed. Also, with the train for Syracuse about due, the ticketseller could have made a natural mistake and given Thurston a ticket to that city.

Whatever applied in this case, I have always attributed the result to wishful thinking on Thurston's part. From boyhood to manhood, his one aim was to become another Herrmann. Just seeing Herrmann's poster was enough to trigger his reaction to the breaking point and from then on, the power of suggestion took full control, building to the climax that came.

This case shows how a matter of a moment can shape an entire lifetime. Everyone recognizes this in physical terms: an individual may victimize himself by simply stepping off a curb without looking for the car that is about to hit him. There the conscious mind is usually responsible, due to some lapse or diversion of attention. Through constant caution, the conscious mind can counteract that trend. Similarly, the unconscious can be controlled to bring out hidden prospects that are otherwise apt to be totally overlooked.

The Thurston case just cited is remarkable purely because a trifling incident was the direct link to a change in career that resulted in a man reaching the very top of his suddenly chosen field. Taking this as a pattern, I quizzed hundreds of people during the course of my tours to learn if any could recall comparable experiences and I found, much to my surprise—and even more to theirs!—that this type of experience was almost universal, although only very few people recognize it.

Some people were literally provoked into a new life by an

incident that seemed unrelated to the final result. One man who began as a clerk in a general store gave special attention to the book department and was promoted to chief clerk with a raise in salary. The company sold out and the buyers decided they didn't need a chief clerk, so they fired him. With no job in sight, he opened a bookstore with his savings; because he had learned to sell books, he was soon outselling the store that had fired him.

In direct contrast, there was a hotel electrician who put so much time and effort into his work that he felt he was indispensible and demanded a substantial raise. When it was refused, he walked off the job, saying he would never work for anybody again. He never did. Having time on his hands, he finished up a few electric gadgets he had promised some friends, found that they wanted more, so he made those as well; almost automatically he found himself in a profitable business of his own.

In many such cases I found evidence of an inner urge that prompted the person's outward action. Yet usually the person did not recognize it, even in retrospect, until many years later, and then only because somebody else's experience caused them to analyze their own. Often the apparent reason for a drastic change seemed totally unrelated to the actual result. The conscious mind has a way of "covering up" for the unconscious, or vice versa. A conscious desire to move from the wintry North to the balmy South can mask the unconscious hope to sell out a Vermont ski resort and buy up a Georgia peanut farm, or vice versa.

Most remarkable of all, I discovered that many people had a series or progression of such experiences, none being very startling, but each having just enough impact to shunt them onto a new course. As a result, they never had a sudden jolt or vivid experience that marked a decided change in a career, because they rarely encountered a situation serious enough to demand it. They had a natural way of cushioning themselves for shocks that lay ahead, but when they looked back, they could usually remember isolated instances that had them worried for a short spell.

That enabled them to recall lesser instances where they had avoided possible problems by recognizing them as they approached or by being on the lookout for them. From this I designed a series of exercises enabling the unconscious to meet such exigencies, both small and large, as well as through different stages of their development. Those exercises follow.

FIRST EXERCISE: MERGING PAST WITH FUTURE

Step One: Use the Contemplation method to induce a stage of deep concentration in which you can visualize a scene from the past or future. Then,

IF FROM THE PAST	IF FROM THE FUTURE
Step Two: Through your power of visual imagery, try to increase your recognition of persons and places involved.	*Step Two:* Focus your mind on the future, trying to visualize things to be in terms of realization.
Step Three: As these impressions develop, implant them in your unconscious mind for purposes of retention. Then:	*Step Three:* Letting such images fade to the retention level, let your retention backtrack to familiar scenes from the past.
Step Four: Skipping the present entirely, project your thoughts to the future, again using visual imagery toward realization of some purpose.	*Step Four:* When you reach a state that calls for increased recognition, develop it in detail through visual imagery.

Step Five: Whichever process you have used so far, you are now ready to merge past with future or vice versa through your power of recall, adding animation through inner-mind expansion, along with other details.

Step Six: During this process you can reject any past ideas that seem too antiquated for future use while strengthening future prospects through adoption of tried-and-true measures.

SECOND EXERCISE: THE FIXED PRESENT

Step One: Using the Contemplation as a mode of concentration, keep your mind fixed firmly on the present as you wait for visual images to develop. Here you have various choices:

Step Two: You can picture yourself (a) at a fork in a road, wondering which way to take, (B) holding a large scale on which you intend to weigh some items, or (c) listening to two people giving you opposite advice.

Step Three: Letting outside impressions form, (a) if they have to do with *past experience,* allocate them to the road on the left, while if they involve *future prospects,* put them on the road to the right; (b) with the scales, visualize yourself weighing them, left for *past,* right for *future;* (c) with two talkers, have one advise staying with what you *already have,* the other going with what you *might get.*

Step Four: Utilize further imagery as well as inner-mind expansion to decide (a) which road to take, (b) which side of the scale has more weight, or (c) which person has won the argument. If the choice is about equal, let it go at that. Then:

Step Five: Take five deep breaths, open your eyes and relax to study your present surroundings as you review the way the choice went and decide upon your own action. In the case of a standoff, you can make another trial at a later date.

THIRD EXERCISE: THE FUTURE PRESENT

This is practically a combination of the previous exercises, so its steps can be given in brief: (1) Proceed as with Merging

Past and Future (Exercise 1). Continue through Steps 2 through 4, but instead of following with Steps 5 and 6 as decision-makers, switch to the Fixed Present (Exercise 2). Picture yourself going through that process at some *future date,* which you can either set immediately or leave for later consideration.

Either way, your next step (5) is to picture yourself at that time, choosing the road, weighing the facts, or listening to arguments, based on the situation as it *will then exist.* This can all be condensed into a single decision-making step (6) since you have already gone through a preliminary visualization leading up to that moment of future decision.

The first exercise is ideal for anyone who has no definite plans or is not pressed for a decision; it amounts to an appraisal that will enable the individual to be alert for things to come. The second exercise can solve an immediate situation such as giving up a job you like for one that pays more money. The third exercise can be a perfect answer for a hectic problem that too often clouds the complex world of today, where a person chases after an opportunity and gets it, only to come home and find that something better was knocking at his door but left while he was gone.

□ 5 □

DILEMMA–SOLVING
BY THE
INNER MIND

One of the most valuable functions of the inner mind is its ability to solve problems that elude the outer mind. The harder you rack your brain, the farther you seem to get from the solution. Relaxation sometimes helps, but too often it serves simply as a breathing spell to fire another surge of brain-racking that leaves your mind more numbed than ever.

Obviously, something more is needed—the unconscious, but you can't strain it like the conscious mind. All the while you are consciously seeking complex solutions, your unconscious is counterbalancing your wasted efforts with such simple terms as *what, why, when, how, where,* and *who.* When those reach the level of the conscious mind, results will be forthcoming. The best way to recognize this is through a brief summary of some outstanding cases, which will serve as patterns that anyone can follow.

■ CASE 1: Fulton Oursler, a noted author, began his literary career as a reporter on a Baltimore newspaper. Among various assignments, he covered a few local concerts, so when the newspaper's music critic was taken ill, he was told to fill in for a brief period. Unfortunately (or fortunately, as it turned out!) Fritz Kreisler, the most celebrated violinist of the time, came to Baltimore just then: and Oursler found himself seated with the veteran music critics of the other Baltimore newspapers.

During the intermission, Oursler listened to the experts exchange comments far beyond his limited experience. When the concert resumed, he listened entranced by Kreisler's music, wondering how he could find terms that would do it justice, let alone fulfill the requirements of his assignment. As he thought in terms of *what* to say, *why* to say it, and so on, he came to the overpowering question: *Who* could say it?

That one word *Who* gave him the answer, straight from the unconscious. As soon as the concert ended, he went to Kreisler's dressing room, told him his problem, and asked if the maestro would be willing to dictate his own impressions of the recital that he had just given. Kreisler was a scholar as well as a musician and this opportunity to become his own critic by proxy immediately intrigued him. He gave Oursler a full review, including special touches that the average critic would have missed and even noting faults that he was sure they had overlooked. When that account appeared under Oursler's name, his dilemma was not merely solved: his reputation as a music critic was made.

Taking this experience as a pattern, you can solve similar dilemmas of your own through the following exercise:

Step One: Start a reverse countdown from fifty to zero to clear your mind of disturbing influences. Gradually focus attention upon the project that you are about to undertake. Then:

Step Two: Picture yourself going through the project in detail, rehearsing it in a calm, easy fashion. Treat this as a sequence or chain of thoughts.

Step Three: Repeat the procedure, link by link, checking each link long enough to decide *how* it should be handled, *why* it is needed, *what* you can do about it; and so on.

Step Four: Review these questions inwardly and if all can be answered satisfactorily, you will be ready to proceed as planned. Otherwise you will have to give special attention to any weak links before going ahead.

Here you have reached the crux of the situation. If you find a weak link that appears beyond repair, you should immediately look for an outside solution based on the link itself. In the case just cited, the missing link occurred with *who,* but it could quite as easily involve *where* or *when* and occasionally some of the other keys already listed. Whatever it proves to be, proceed as follows:

Step Five: Focus your visualization on the new lead. If *who,* picture yourself speaking to that person. If *where,* picture yourself in the place involved. If *when,* picture yourself at that time.

Step Six: Simply develop the picture from that point on. The new sequence will provide its own answers. Try it and you will find out.

In discussing the dilemma factor with people who have encountered it, I have found that if they simply follow those first four steps, they will immediately know just how they stand—whether to proceed on their own or to seek an answer from another source. One college student told me: "I was beginning to flunk exams because I thought I had the answers to things I didn't really know. When I tried your system of quizzing myself to start, it was like a whole new ballgame. I checked all the tough answers first and the rest fell in line."

I also met a woman who had a remarkable flair for prompting social events on a lavish and attractive scale, but invariably they bogged down because somebody failed to come through as promised, or there was a conflict of dates or a lack of necessary accommodations. She was ready to give up what should have been a profitable business when I told her: "Your trouble is that you think only in terms of 'what, why, and how' when you should be concentrating on 'who, when, and where.' Give those first preference and the others will fall into line." She did and she is still in business.

■ CASE 2: At times, finding yourself strictly "on your own" can more than double your dilemma. This is the classic example of a noted statesman, Chauncey Depew, who during his twelve years as a United States senator from New York was regarded as one of the greatest orators of his time.

On one occasion, Senator Depew accepted the simplest of commitments—to make a speech at an important political convention. Pressed by other work, he put off writing his speech until just before the convention; then, suddenly, he found himself without a theme. Here was the case of a man faced by a dilemma which he alone could solve, for he was the one person to whom everyone else came when they found themselves totally at loss for words!

As Depew sat on the veranda of his country club overlooking the Hudson River in the bright glare of a summer sun, his thoughts went blank and the dazzling view itself faded into the interior of the convention hall, with which he was familiar. He saw a chairman he did not know; he saw a man named Quigg make a motion for the nomination of candidates; and he saw himself rise in response and deliver the speech for which he was actually unprepared! As he listened, he felt an increasing glow of satisfaction that culminated when the sea of faces blended back into the glittering scene of the familiar Hudson River.

Almost automatically Chauncey Depew arose, went to his room, and wrote out the speech exactly as his inner mind had heard it. He delivered it at the convention hall in Saratoga with full confidence that it would be applauded—which it was—because he recognized the unknown chairman he had seen during his mental projection; and the man who called upon Depew for the nominating speech was none other than Mr. Quigg.

Fantastic? Far from it! I have personally gone through similar experiences, wondering what I was going to do or say for a group of people who were wondering what I was going to do or say. Always I followed the same rule: I projected myself into the situation and went on from there. You can do the same. Just think ahead to the thing you want to do and you may find it already done. Results should be rapidly forthcoming if you follow this procedure:

Begin with the preliminary exercise as given in Steps 1 to 4 in order to establish your exact purpose. Whenever you recognize that the answer to your problem lies within your own ability, ignore Steps 5 and 6 as already given (page 76) and switch to these,

Step Five A: Picture yourself *completing* whatever purpose you have in mind: closing a sale, winning a game, receiving a bonus or an award, accepting a new job, or whatever your aim may be. Establish that as a *fixed fact,* turning the *future* into the *present.*

Step Six A: Now let your thoughts drift back in retrospect. Imagine yourself recalling the details of your upward climb. You can be telling people about it, even noting their reactions until you reach the climax, which should be the very picture with which you started.

You can repeat these steps several times, even embellishing them and picturing points you overlooked. The more satisfaction you gain, the more you expand upon the theme, the more realistic it becomes. What you are doing is establishing a future effort as a past achievement, turning speculation into actuality or something closely resembling it. This does not mean that you can predict the future, but you can often help shape it through confidence and attention to detail. The closer you come to your pictorial target through the exercise just outlined, the more you will increase your chance of success.

■ CASE 3: There is still another form of dilemma that demands special consideration. Where the two just mentioned may involve intuition this can tap the realm of inspiration, moving from mere objectivity into creativity, where the unconscious takes full control. A noted church organist, Lewis W. Redner, was given the words of a new Christmas poem and asked to put the verses to music. This was not an unusual assignment, but in this instance the words haunted him to such a degree that no music seemed adequate to accompany the verse, and on the evening before the scheduled rehearsal he reviewed all his efforts to no avail and went to sleep hoping to make a last-minute try the next morning.

During the night he awoke hearing a soft voice singing an angelic strain that fitted the verse to perfection. He jotted down the tune as his mind kept repeating it, and in the morning he filled in the harmony; the song was rehearsed as scheduled. With the years that song, "O, Little Town of Bethlehem," has become one of the most popular of modern Christmas carols.

Such experiences are by no means uncommon, but their importance is generally overlooked because the desired result is usually attained before a person's mental tension approaches the breaking point. Whenever your conscious mind tries to put things together like a jigsaw puzzle, your unconscious picks up the discarded pieces and gets into the game on its own. Since they are working independently, the harder you drive your conscious mind, the more you are depending on your unconscious to deliver what the conscious won't or can't.

When trifling matters are involved, the net result is often simple, yet deceptive. The conscious mind, working on its own, becomes bored or annoyed when results are not forthcoming and either takes a breather or turns to other matters. That gives the unconscious a chance to "speak for itself" in a quiet, subtle way, so that when the conscious mind gets back to the problem, it finds the answer waiting for it and promptly takes the credit.

The proper course is to work steadily and methodically with the conscious mind, letting the unconscious take over at specified intervals, giving it equal time with the conscious. That is the part that most people neglect, particularly after they have had a few lucky breaks as a result of the unconscious bobbing up with a few timely ideas. Two points are essential: (1) The conscious mind must supply the unconscious with sufficient material to work with. (2) The unconscious must be given an opportunity to report back fully with its findings.

There you have the basis for the following exercise:

Steps One to Four: Go through the usual procedure to determine the status of the project: whether it might require outside aid or research; if not, you must decide whether it is routine or inspirational.

These preliminary steps are vital in this case, because often an inspirational theme may involve some other person; and there are also times when routine and inspiration can become intermingled. From there, continue with:

Step Five B: Mentally keep listing ideas, materials, ingredients, or whatever might be required for your purpose, comparing and rejecting them or keeping them for future reference. Then:

Step Six B: Clear your mind with a simple countdown and wait for ideas to develop. Don't cut this short; if given time, some impressions may grow and clarify while others may dwindle.

Step Seven B: Instead of merely repeating Step 5B, continue on, letting your unconscious suggestions inspire new areas of conscious thought. This adds a *progressive* feature not found in other types of exercise.

Step Eight B: Again clear your thoughts for another dip into the unconscious, during which you balance previous impressions. Picture them like objects being weighed against one another or studied in some other selective fashion.

Step Nine B: This can best be described as a merger of the conscious and the unconscious, with an exchange of ideas like two people completing a jigsaw puzzle together. Here the picture takes final shape, either gradually or suddenly— dependent somewhat on the nature of the project but always with a sense of certainty.

I have made a special study of experiences of this type, with some very unusual findings. Writers, lecturers, and composers can all naturally cite instances along this line. They are apt to have ideas bob up from nowhere like a "bolt from the blue" because they are constantly thinking in such terms. But I have found that people who follow the step-by-step process just outlined not only get results more surely and with less strain but are also able to apply their aptitude to many phases of daily life; in fact, I have patterned my formula on the results of my survey.

There was James Galbry, a candy manufacturer, who made mental tours of his factory, picturing improvements or ways to increase production. Often he was surprised by the accuracy of his visualization and he was pleased when key employees would sometimes give him the very suggestions he had imagined they would. He visualized sales meetings in the same manner; whenever business lagged, he tried to synchronize three factors in his mind: the plant, the product, and promotion.

On one such tour, the workers seemed too busy to notice him and he saw big cartons being stacked on a loading platform. He heard people laughing about somebody named "JoJo." He decided to switch his thoughts to a sales meeting. He stopped to pick up a candy bar from a belt line and was starting to eat it when he entered the meeting room where the sales manager was waving to a big display and was saying, "I hoped you'd get here first, Mr. Galbry, to see the JoJo display before anybody else."

"JoJo?" echoed Galbry. "Who is JoJo?"

"Who is JoJo?" laughed the sales manager. "You should say, 'What is JoJo?' You should know. You're eating one."

Unconsciously, so Galbry told me, he studied the display, detail by detail. It showed a package he had never seen before:

THE   JOJO   BAR

GALBRY'S   GREATEST

THE   TASTE   TELLS

Galbry looked at the candy bar. It was different from any they had made before. He bit into it, it was richer and thicker in chocolate, something he had talked about quite often. With that, Galbry came back to reality. No JoJo; no belt lines working overtime to fill up loading platforms with a product that wasn't even displayed. None of those—right then. Three months later they were all a reality, with the factory buzzing like it never had before, with thousands of customers buying and eating JoJo Bars and saying that Galbry had done it again, which he had.

Kay Ray was a very resourceful woman who had a knack of analyzing problems and finding the answers by following the formulas given in this chapter. She hit her peak when her daughter Carolyn came home unexpectedly from college and received a last-minute invitation to attend a fancy dress ball that was the big event of the local social season. Carolyn had always wanted to attend one of those gala affairs and had even dreamed of wearing a fancy dress that would gain honorable mention. Some of the participants spent weeks of time and hundreds of dollars preparing their costumes and familiarizing themselves with the ways of characters they were supposed to represent.

With only a day to go, Carolyn didn't even have time for a hairdo to go with a rented costume, if she could find such a costume anywhere in town. Carolyn was ready to cancel the date, but Kay said "No" and began to concentrate on the problem. She immediately eliminated any ideas of outside aid; there was no one *who* could supply it, no place *where* it could come from, while the question of *when* was right now, with no time to waste.

Kay obviously had to depend on her own devices, and since she had never been faced with such a situation, it couldn't be treated as a routine based upon past experience. That put it in the inspirational realm, so Kay breezed through the first four steps and finally concentrated on Carolyn as the belle of the ball. Kay pictured herself going through the house to find *what* to use and *how* to use it. The question of *why* was still a factor, because until Kay took a mental inventory of *what* was available, she wouldn't be able to decide upon the costume; during her mental tour she also reverted briefly to *who* and *where* in case she had to call on neighbors to supply something she didn't have.

The break came when Kay thought of an India print that she was using as a bedspread in the spare room. By picturing it as a sari, Kay solved the question of Carolyn's dark hair, which could be combed straight back and formed into a bun. Now that India was becoming the motif, Kay's thoughts turned to a box of junk jewelry that she had been gathering for a charity bazaar, then she recalled an old travel magazine with color photos of India showing people in their native garb. She promptly assembled all those items—and more, for the travel pictures showed a Hindu blouse that closely resembled a nylon jersey top—and Kay's sewing basket provided a sparkling sequin for Carolyn's forehead, to go with her array of necklaces and bracelets. A supply of suntan powder left over from the previous summer added the final touch, and Carolyn emerged as the exact counterpart of the Maharanee of Tongore, whose picture had appeared on the magazine cover in full regalia.

Carolyn's escort scarcely recognized her when he arrived in a cavalier's costume and when Kay retired early, she left a note on the living room table, saying, "Put it right here." It was there the next morning: a silver loving cup that Carolyn had won as the grand prize for the most original costume.

Many more cases could be cited, furnishing a surprising number of variations, results of the individual purposes of the persons involved. Always, the twin factors of concentration and autosuggestion are present, with one taking over where the other leaves off, so that it sometimes becomes difficult to tell one from the other. Sometimes these merge with a dream state, or a person may approach a stage of deep contemplation, but those factors may be due to the importance of the problem or the sudden way in which the solution comes to mind.

The common denominator in all cases is the time element, though it is not always recognizable as such. Sometimes you can sense a dilemma soon enough to start working on it before the pressure begins, so it is a good plan to cultivate that practice. Begin your day by thinking ahead to things that need attention, to learn if you have been dismissing them simply because they are unimportant or whether you have been avoiding them because they may confront you with questions that you are not yet ready to answer. That way, you can properly eliminate anything that is really unimportant and at the same time get a head start before an actual problem becomes too pressing.

□ THE ART OF DAYDREAMING □

Daydreaming is a normal phenomenon. Years ago, its importance was minimized, even by behaviorists. We know that the dreams we have while sleeping are vital to psychological health, since they often serve as a kind of release for our tensions, worries, concerns, interests, and the like. As it turns out, so does daydreaming. It is proving to be an intrinsic and important part of our daily life, and a certain amount of daydreaming each day seems essential for retaining equilibrium. Not that you should spend all your time in a dream world, but psychologists are beginning to find that certain amounts of daydreaming result in improved self-control and an enhanced creative thinking ability; it can be an impetus for improving upon reality, and it becomes a powerful spur towards achievement.

Many people in business report that daydreaming helps them recall tasks, obligations and objectives they forget in the daily press of practical concerns. At times, daydreaming can become like a mental vacation, changing one's pace and thinking, leaving one more relaxed and refreshed, even more optimistic and enthusiastic and filled with purpose. It tends often to heighten the senses; colors seem brighter and more intense and objects seem to take on a greater depth. It can become another way of solving everyday problems, and a way of coming up more readily with new ideas. As a matter of fact, constant conscious effort to solve a problem is sometimes the most inefficient way of tackling it. When you try to solve a problem, you often tend to create tension, so that if you are not able to relax or to "let go" of a problem you are very often preventing its solution.

Newton was famous for his private reflections, as was Thomas Alva Edison, who thought nothing of stretching out in his workshop to let fantasies flood his mind, or just let his thoughts wander. Debussy used to gaze at the River Seine; Dostoevski would often doodle; Brahms found ideas came effortlessly when he was deeply daydreaming. César Franck walked in a dreamlike daze while composing. John Dewey spoke of his own reverie as important to creative work. Pole-vaulting champ John Uleses deliberately used daydreaming to reconstruct a scene—a future scene—of winning. Harry S. Truman claimed he used daydreaming for rests and recuperation—he termed it "the fox-hole in my mind." Conrad Hilton claimed that all of his accomplishments were first realized in his imagination. The humanistic thinker Dr. Harry Emerson Fosdick was aware of the tremendous power of daydreaming. He said, "Hold a picture of yourself long and steadily enough in your mind's eye, and you will be drawn towards it. Picture yourself vividly as defeated, and that alone will make victory impossible; picture yourself as winning, and that will contribute immeasurably to success. Do not picture yourself as anything, and you will drift like a derelict."

The reader may, after a while, find a mental escape trip a favorite way to travel, without having to make airplane reservations, talk to a travel bureau, or find a car or bus, and with little or no traffic. By using your imagination, you can learn to find a place where you can feel safe, secure and free, where nothing can harm you; you can feel good and may even want to make up variations of this trip, so that in moments of stress, when you have a chance to escape to another room, or to the back of a bus, you can make this trip. It might be a magic carpet, on which you fly all over the world to your favorite places; you might be a deep-sea scuba diver and swim among the coral forests and the tropical fish; it may be a favorite scene or place where you have been before; but it is the kind of thing that could be just an ideal reservation to hold in the back of your mind whenever you wish to fantasize for a few minutes and go on a relaxation trip. You might wish to imagine yourself on a beach where the sand is white and the ocean is calm and sparkling and the warm sun is sinking right into your bones. You will enjoy this feeling for awhile, or you may walk through a forest, enjoying the lush greens and exotic flowers and the beauty of the sky, the softness of the air. Regarding your favorite place, you should fill in the details, painting mental pictures—what's the scenery like, the aromas, the sounds, the weather, what are your feelings. You can almost experience this place in your imagination and will experience it as vividly as you can. You might pretend you are reporting about it, or making a movie about it; consequently, you are fixing the details in your mind and, when you have enjoyed it fully, you can slowly return to the real world and open your eyes.

□ 6 □
DECISION-MAKING EXERCISES

These techniques fall into three categories that will be treated in chronological order: (1) *Basic,* where situations may be anticipated while they are forming; (2) *Advanced,* where a situation has already developed and a decision must be made accordingly; and (3) *Ultimate,* where the situation itself demands attention and an issue is being forced upon the person involved. Though all three have points of similarity, each requires its own technique.

First Exercise: BASIC
During Formative Stage

This exercise is of prime importance to people with varied interests, because they can make it virtually a part of their daily lives. It can be applied to any simple decision to which you are not yet fully committed. This is the type of decision that has to do with the present; if you practice the exercise frequently with small dilemmas, you will find it highly effective when you deal with larger questions.

Step One: Read the instructions carefully; then half-close your eyes and begin a slow countdown from 50 to zero. By the time you reach 40, let your inner impressions blend into:

Step Two: Form a mental image of *yourself,* closing your eyes to help it develop further. It can be like the reflection in a mirror, or you can see yourself in action as in a home movie or as a still portrait.

Step Three: End the counting as you concentrate on yourself. Picture yourself in contrasting situations. Treat yourself as *two different persons:* one on the left, the other on the right. As an example: *On the left,* YOU are considering certain prospects or advantages you could gain from a new job or environment; *on the right,* YOU are picturing how to make the most out of what you already have established or planned. Tab these mentally:

YOU—*On Left*	YOU—*On Right*
Better surroundings in living, working, or both.	Already planning to improve general conditions.
Increased responsibilities, more demands on time.	Time is your own, with helpers to handle details.
New social contacts—added outside interests—recreation and/or vacation trips.	Old friends of long standing. Few but with mutual interests. Occasionally get together.
Higher costs, rent, entertaining, transportation, with due allowance for same.	Income well budgeted, with cuts possible if needed. Any extras unlikely.
Opportunities for promotion or work in specialized fields with promise of reward.	Chance of growing with business or gaining importance in community.

Step Four: After checking out such listed items or whatever might apply in your individual case, picture yourself acting out the parts, both left and right—still as two personalities:

YOU—*On Left*	YOU—*On Right*
You are relaxing, enjoying your new surroundings. Phone bells begin to ring, burdening you with details. You have subordinates but they are all busy, too.	You are very bored. Same old office, still waiting for delivery of new equipment. Better take afternoon off; somebody else can handle anything that comes up.
You check your week's calendar and decide to drop from golf tournament or call off ski trip. Must attend sales conference—chairman of the board will be there.	You call friends to arrange a golf game. One is out of town, another not feeling well. Nobody wants to go bowling. You go home to watch television.
Going through expense accounts. Okay some, hold others until later. Call home; won't be there for dinner. Have to work on special regarding new projects. One month late.	Good news in evening. Phone call regarding company merger. If it goes through, plant may expand. Property values will go up all over town—including yours.

NOTE: Try to be impartial in these picturizations, letting one lead into another so they represent a time lapse of several months or more. If you feel optimistic to start, try to become reasonably apprehensive; if you are pessimistic, try to brighten up a bit. Be yourself—or rather *yourselves*, both of them!

Step Five: This combines concentration with confrontation between yourselves. Keep stressing that you are *two entities* (which should be easy, now that you have gone this far) and simply bring them together. Treat it as a chance meeting or renewal of a passing acquaintance. Be impersonal as you switch back and forth, letting each tell the other of his problems and getting suggestions in response.

Step Six: Having completed the dialogue in which ideas have been exchanged between your two selves, go over it mentally to keep the important points in mind. Then return each self to the starting point and visualize them as they should be now, basing each course of action on suggestions from the other.

For example:

YOU—*On Left*	YOU—*On Left*
No telephones ringing today. Helpers are taking calls so that you can hold a meeting finalizing your special report on new projects in order to present it to the chairman of the board during the sales conference.	Your work is so well ahead of schedule that you are taking a week's vacation. During your absence your office is to be renovated as already planned.
You have approved all expense accounts and are requisitioning more to take chairman on trip to ski resort to set dates for launching of new projects. Your secretary is calling your home to say that you will be there for dinner.	You will be gone on a fishing trip with friends you met while playing alone on the local golf links. Immediately after your return you will recommend that your company consider bids for the construction of a new plant in anticipation of a coming merger.

Step Seven: Having revised your schedule of activities according to the recommendations of your other self, you are now in a better position to decide which course you should take. If you are still undecided, form a mental picture of a big scale on which you can put various advantages and balance them up, left and right. Whichever way the scale tips is likely to be best for you, but if it tends to waver back and forth, it may well be that neither is suitable and you should look for something in between.

Second Exercise: ADVANCED
During Conflict Stage

After passing the basic stage, you can continue viewing yourself in contrasting situations until you approach the advanced stage, where such comparisons may prove difficult or impossible. Until you have formed an opinion, you have to shift back and forth from one self to the other during the formative period. But unless you can balance your opinions to some degree, tossing them back and forth between your selves, you will stifle the interchange of ideas that produces harmonious relations between the two and your opinions will become one-sided. This can cause a conflict between the outer and inner selves, when one tends to represent the type of person you feel you *should be* and the other the type you really *want to be*.

As this develops, the outer self becomes the opinion-maker, going along with whatever seems best for your chosen purpose or career. The crisis comes when this reaches a stage where your inner self has no voice at all and is ready to tear down all that your outer self has built up. To appreciate this situation, you must first recognize it, which you can do through the following exercise:

Step One: Consider yourself impersonally as you review your present situation. If you feel that you are like two people in conflict, weigh each thus:

OUTER SELF	INNER SELF
When and why did your present outer self begin its takeover?	Did your inner self of that period argue the point then?
Did you act on the advice or suggestion of another person?	Did anyone encourage you to follow your inner notions?
Can you recall further factors that strengthened your decision?	Did you have chances to revert to your earlier ideas?
Are outside factors now responsible for your adherence to your aim?	Have you purposely avoided anyone or anything that would turn you back?

Step Two: Put the situation in direct reverse, picturing what might have happened if your two selves had played opposite parts.

OUTER SELF (As Inner Self)	INNER SELF (As Outer Self)
Could you still have voiced opinions if you had let your other self assume control?	Would you have accepted such opinions or advice?
What have you missed by having your own way?	What do you think you could have gained if you had taken over?
Are former friends or advisors satisfied with your results, or not?	Has advice you ignored turned out better than you believed it would?
Would your home life have been greatly improved?	Would whatever you might have gained be worth it?

Step Three: Your next process is to merge these conflicting opinions into what can be termed the *composite self,* interweaving the answers to your mental queries to form a new outlook based on the realities of today. If you have fully established yourself in one field, you can't very well shift to another extreme and begin all over, but you can adapt yourself to changed conditions. On the contrary, new or unforeseen commitments may demand your entry into a field you had hitherto avoided—such as a college professor being called upon to run for a political office—and there this advanced form of decision-making takes on vital importance.

Third Exercise: ULTIMATE
During Final Stage

Don't let the term *ultimate* deceive you into thinking that you may be dealing with something a long way off. You have met many people who reached the ultimate stage of a career with the first job they ever took simply because they stayed with it and continued to advance in a steady, satisfying way, sometimes to their own disadvantage. Others have found themselves precipitated into such a situation without realizing it, while many have marked a crossroad where they could have taken one turn or the other. Sometimes we act blindly or too trustingly when confronted with an ultimate decision. The purpose of this section is to help you avoid such pitfalls.

Step One: Clear your mind of all thoughts except those of yourself and your surroundings as you begin a countdown from 50 to zero. Try to see yourself as a mirror image while you count.

Step Two: Make the image more realistic by having it *count with you.* At any time, you can go back and start the count all over, your aim being to have your image take over and do the counting on its own.

Step Three: Drop the counting and let your image *speak for itself.* You won't find this uncanny; instead, it should be natural, because you want your *inner self* to tell your *outer self* that you are both doing well for both your selves—that is, YOU.

Step Four: Consider your assets, your studies, or your job. Your prospects, as they stand or should stand. Friends, contacts, finances. Outside interests, including hobbies. Anything related to self-improvement.

Step Five: The parting of the ways. Review all items and classify them under these heads:

Established	*Projected*
Phases of your life essential to your present status or that can be used to improve or advance it along established lines. Consider factors that will increase your efficiency while strengthening your position.	Here you put anything that can or could be used in some effective, worthwhile way outside your established routine. Try to group these items toward a mutual purpose or common end.

Step Six: Appraise the two listings. Any item belonging to both can be listed in each column. The others are weighed as follows:

Established	*Projected*
Put established factors into practice while reducing extra effort and eliminating unnecessary items. Keep any that promise expansion or could mean promotion along established lines. Neglect nothing but don't be wasteful.	Anything subtracted from the established side can be added here if good enough to keep. Shift new ideas to the established side if needed there. Otherwise, keep building toward a projected purpose.

Step Seven: Final decision. Here the picture broadens. With two courses opening before you, each drawing from the other, an in-between prospect will invariably present itself, giving you three choices:

Established	*Opportunity*	*Projected*
Keep this as a symbol of the past, to help set a future standard. Picture conditions as they could be, or should be, if everyone cooperated. Think in terms of new ideas supplanting old, toward increased efficiency. Visualize attitudes of your associates and your own moods as well. Treat your existing situation and surroundings as though your life depended on them—which it might! At the same time be ready to shake off shackles.	This is a definite reflection of your present mood, likely to change from day to day. Dismiss random notions and try to link past results to future prospects. Relaxation is important here, and new contracts are advisable if they can soften past problems or produce future benefits. Picture a scale on which you weigh old items against new. An exact balance is a time for action!	Here you must visualize the future in *present* terms, just as you did with the past. Anything on which you have depended to maintain your equilibrium—routine, security, associates, surroundings—should be pictured to the last detail, with no room for doubt. Picture yourself *as you were* in comparison with yourself *as you will be*. When both sides tally in all essential points, you can consider a changeover, if one offers as much as or more than the other.

In analyzing countless cases involving decision-making and advising people as to which exercises will best fulfill their individual needs, I have found that the ultimate technique, properly applied, can meet almost every known need. The pitfall here is that many people either utilize it too soon or wait until too late; in both cases, they expect results too fast. Until you are reasonably sure of a fixed type of work or profession, with sufficient contacts to guarantee that your services will be in continued demand, there is no use in planning for an alternative, for if your established expectations are on the verge of collapse your projected plans will be ready to go with them. So you will need a basic rather than an ultimate exercise.

Similarly, some people are apt to class themselves as established simply because they are mired in a rut so deep that nobody has gone to the trouble to pry them out of it. Anyone who has passed the formative stage should drop the basic for an advanced exercise to get rid of any conflicts before moving on to the final stage of the ultimate.

Let's take a few examples to show exactly how the ultimate approach has functioned and how you can profit from it.

■ CASE 1: *Established to Projected* John Thomas was a magazine editor, a good one. His job was twofold: to appraise writers and to encourage them. To do that, he let them have their way, then made recommendations concerning the course he felt they should follow. As a result, he became the "literary father" to a group of rising writers. Not only was he famous for discovering new writers, he developed new editors to take over when he retired, which he did much sooner than people expected. During an extended vacation he discovered a remarkable new writer: himself. His first novel was a best-seller and all that followed were equally successful. In telling others what to do he had learned how much more he could do and had turned his *established* self into his *projected* self.

■ CASE 2: *Established to Projected to Established*   Jack Bart was advertising chief for a large department store. His small but well-trained staff operated like clockwork, giving him time to take up outdoor sports and become an authority on such subjects, delivering talks that grew into profitable lectures. The management approved Bart's sideline as good public relations for the store, never realizing how big this outside activity had grown until Bart tendered his resignation as advertising chief. The store owner sent for him in amazement, wanting to know the trouble, for until then Bart had seemed the most satisfied man on the entire staff.

Bart explained his decision quite simply. He had not asked for a raise because he was already getting a salary that was higher than the job was worth. So he had upped his lecture rates and pushed new contacts in that field until it was bringing him an annual income equal to his job as ad chief. He was making the shift from one to the other, confident that he could double his income by devoting full time to his lectures alone.

"And how long would that take?" asked the store owner.

"At least a year," replied Bart, "maybe two. Yes, I'm sure I can do it in two years."

"And I can do it for you in two minutes," announced the store owner, reaching for the telephone. "I'm calling the business department to have them double your next paycheck. Any man who can make as much on the outside as he does working for us is worth that much more to our store. I'll find things for you to do that will make up the difference."

The store owner did that and more. He put Jack Bart to work bringing other departments up to the standard of efficiency he had set for his own. Within the next few years Bart had become the store's general manager with a salary five times the amount he had received as advertising chief. By proving his worth as his *projected* self, Jack Bart had gained recognition for his *established* self, something he had deserved all along.

■ CASE 3:   Charles Darrow had a job that was about as good as any job during the Depression years. He had already seen the need for switching from an *established* situation into a *projected* field and had considered real estate as a logical choice, but now that market had suffered a collapse, leaving him wondering what to do with his spare time.

Having skill as a designer and a decided flair for real estate, Darrow decided to combine the two into an asset in the form of a new table game. At least it enabled him to forget his own problems, if only temporarily. By the time he had completed the game and was beginning to market it, he was able to forget those problems permanently. Not only did millions of people buy it, they did so through the succeeding generations who are still buying it today. That game was Monopoly. It stands as a prime example of what can happen when *established* and *projected* purposes are creatively merged.

□ 7 □

CONTEMPLATION
Probing Your Hidden Power

Concentration is an *active* factor in mind development; contemplation is a *passive* factor. Concentration represents *intensity*, contemplation supplies *relaxation*. By alternating regularly and judiciously, you can find a balance point in mind development that will enable you to acquire unity along with effort. Once you recognize how one leads into the other, you will be able to begin with either, thus gaining proficiency in both.

In that way you can merge the *facts* of the past with the *fantasy* of the future, to form the *realism* of the present. That's why I like the story an old professor told me about how he would have liked to bring a student from the past to meet his counterpart from the future in the present, only to find that they wouldn't agree—each would have been concentrating on making the other see things his way. If each had been concentrating on the other's problems instead of his own, things might have worked out differently; but in that case they could have gone too far the other way, which is just as bad.

Facts from the past are true, but they count only so far as

you have learned them or experienced them. The future is sure to come, but you can shape it only within the limitations of your own scope or ability. The one thing you can control and expand, if you put your mind to it, is the present; that can be done through *contemplation*—which represents the balance point between the past and future and thereby enables you to make the most of all your concentrated effort in those two fields through contemplation.

The time factor is so important in everyone's mind development that I like to picture it as an hourglass, the top compartment filled with sand, representing the past, with its grains trickling through the narrow central passage that stands for the present, gradually filling the lower portion that signifies the future. For some persons, particularly in bygone days, this slow process could take an entire lifetime, during which past experiences were gradually built into future prospects; for others there was more progress, so that the hourglass could be turned over at intervals, marking a change in purpose or the start of a new career.

Today, things move more rapidly. You may find that a whole backlog of accumulated knowledge can be poured into future achievement, with each turn of the glass marking a step to new attainment. The key to that is found in one word: *association.* How association combines concentration with contemplation will be covered in the pages that follow.

☐ GROUP ASSOCIATION ☐

EXERCISE NUMBER ONE

Here you will focus your mind on a single object and from it form a list of items directly associated with it according to specified categories. This can be done mentally, as a practice exercise; for more definitive results, use pencil and paper to compile a full list as you proceed.

Step One: Read the instructions carefully so that you can follow them in detail. Within the steps are different stages, and each stage can be treated as a new test.

Step Two: With pencil and paper handy, start a simple time count, running up to approximately thirty seconds (page 6). As you do, concentrate on a single object, in this case a tree. This is to be your over-all target through all stages of the exercise.

Step Three: When you complete the count, close your eyes and visualize the complete tree. If necessary, repeat the count to gain a stronger visual image. Do not use a countdown; you are to build an image, not melt it away.

Step Four: This is the beginning of *stage 1.* With the tree in mind, keep visualizing it from top to bottom and even below, listing every detail you see. Open and close your eyes at intervals, noting the features in whatever sequence they occur.

Step Five: This is a check of Step 4, with a few more details. Keep your eyes open as you name parts of the tree, but close them to visualize such parts more fully as well as to visualize any unusual item you feel should be added to complete your contemplation.

Step Five: This is the beginning of *stage 2.* Maintaining the image of the tree, do a countdown from 50 to zero (page 15). Here you are *reversing* your imagery, but instead of concentrating on a melting process, picture the tree fading from view as it falls apart. As this happens, you can forget the count and focus on the various uses to which the wood can be put.

Step Six: *Concentrate* just enough to picture items forming so that you can *contemplate* them and compile a new list. Again, you can deal in words with eyes open, or you can work with images, with eyes closed until you list them. If this carries your mind far afield, go along with it into:

Step Seven: Add items to the list as long as they come easily and bear a reasonably close relationship to the original tree. Otherwise, use this step as a final checkup of products you have already itemized.

Step Eight: This is the beginning of *stage 3,* an optional procedure. Simply recreate the image of the tree with a simple count to thirty seconds, but think of it as a *whole* and classify it as a particular species, beginning a new list with its name.

Step Nine: Picture the tree, turning to another species, then another, and so on, listing them all. You may have to group some in special classes, visualizing them; for others, names alone may suffice. Some knowledge of trees is helpful here; if you are totally unfamiliar with tree classification, you may forego this third stage. With all you may have heard or read about trees, however, it is a good plan to see how many names you can come up with.

Now comes the remarkable part of this exercise. Refer to pages 106–107; you will find itemized lists compiled during the three stages by a person who decided to try the exercise, thinking that the target word *tree* would produce a reasonable number of responses, only to be amazed by the size of the list as well as its variety. But what concerns you most is this: How many of those words were in your mind to start with and how many began springing up as you went along, almost from nowhere? Thinking back, you will probably agree that the list seemed to grow of its own accord as you went along, and that brings up another question.

Taking specific words that rather surprised you when you listed them, how long ago was it that you used some particular word—or heard or read it? Chances are you won't have any idea as to the time, except that it was a long way back. Why should you have thought of those words at all? The answer is plain: through association. Most people are aware that association plays an important part in their daily lives, but they confine it to simple terms, usually in pairs—salt and pepper, bread and butter, meat and potatoes, knife and fork, rose and thorn. These lead nowhere, except to suggest such phrases as:

"On the spur of the moment," when you came through with the solution to a problem nobody else could answer.

"In the twinkling of an eye," when something happened so fast that you alone could describe it.

"It was now or never," which became a moment of truth that was finally shortened to "This is it."

"Up a tree," which puts you out on a limb like a possum waiting for a lot of barking dogs to go away.

That brings us right back to that one word *tree*. Instead of being limited to paired associations, it provided the key to as many as one hundred. Why? Because you were dealing in groups. Beginning with a small cluster of ideas, anything related to those naturally became part of their category. Things didn't just pair up; they became part of a conglomerate.

□ GROUP ASSOCIATION □

EXERCISE NUMBER TWO

In the preceding exercise in word associations, the groups represented by each stage consisted of (1) *components,* (2) *products,* and (3) *types.* In this exercise, the second stage has been eliminated and the order of the other two reversed. Otherwise, it follows much the same pattern, giving you a further opportunity to appreciate how great a vocabulary you have already acquired without realizing it. To further that purpose, we will use two closely related target words, one for each stage: *house* and *home.*

Step One: Prepare for this exercise, as in the previous one, by reading the instructions and then proceeding with each stage separately.

Step Two: This is the beginning of *stage 1,* since you will be using the target word *house* in this stage alone. Close your eyes and begin a simple time count, up to thirty seconds, or more if needed. As you count, envision a simple house, *exterior only.* If you wish, you can pause, open your eyes, and draw the house in simple outline. Otherwise, simply fix it in mind.

Step Three: With or without a further time count, imagine the house changing in size of shape, into a *different type* of abode: large or small, ancient or modern, primitive or lavish. Write down a word that describes it, whether the dwelling of a prince or a peasant, then let it change into another and list that as well.

Step Four: Continue the process, opening your eyes as much as you wish, thinking simply in words at times, but adding images if they help to increase the list. No need to continue counting unless you become too firmly fixed on one impression; then you can do a countdown to clear your mind and make a fresh start. When your list lags, terminate it.

NOTE: Think of these exteriors in terms of countries or climate; of the people who built them; anything, simple or elaborate, that will expand your list.

Step Five: This is the beginning of *stage 2*. Switch to your other target word, *home*. Here you also use a simple time count—from one second to thirty or beyond—while imagining that you are entering a house and viewing the interior. Your purpose is to identify each room or portion of the home *by name*, as you picture it. Use a simple listing of rooms found in many homes. Then:

Step Six: Picture and try to name rooms or apartments you would see in more elaborate homes, including those you may have read about or seen in movies. Add outlying portions of the home if any occur to you, switching from one type of home to another, extending names and pictures to your utmost limit.

After concluding your lists, turn to page 107 and check the items you find there, just as you did with Exercise 1. Again, your list should surprise you; you may also be intrigued by some you missed, particularly any that you immediately recognize upon reading them.

☐ GROUP ASSOCIATION ☐

EXERCISE NUMBER THREE

This involves a single target, with only one stage, but for convenience it has been given a double name that describes it very aptly: *streets* and *alleys*. In Colonial times, that just about described the makeup of every town and most cities; in fact, those terms persisted strongly through the horse-and-buggy days. With the coming of the automobile with municipal improvements extending to the suburbs and beyond, new terms have been devised from street and alley; some are highly descriptive, others a matter of prestige. Grouping them is the purpose of this exercise.

Step One: Picture yourself moving about town, looking at street signs or hunting for addresses—all involving names other than street or alley—any that you may have heard or read about. List them as you go along. Then:

Step Two: Carry your quest out into the country, noting names on the road map as you drive along. From there, imagine that you are strolling along on foot, or riding a bicycle or a horse, to see what other names you encounter among the country roads.

As before, check your results with those shown on page 108. This list, too, can produce surprises in the form of associations that never would have occurred to you if you hadn't tried to group them. This not only shows the power of association, it also gives you a pattern you can follow in similar exercises of your own. Simply pick a target word that offers possibilities of expansion and proceed in the fashion already outlined, drawing upon the hidden reserve of words and ideas you have been building unaware.

☐ GROUP ASSOCIATION KEY LIST ☐

EXERCISE 1—STAGE 1
TREE: trunk, limb, bough, branch, twig, leaf, stem, *bark,* roots, sap, *syrup,* buds, blossom, *fruit, nut,* seed, *cones, needles.*

EXERCISE 1—STAGE 2
TREE (products): logs, lumber, sawdust, board, stake, firewood, kindling, flooring, paneling, roofing, beams, posts, doors, furniture, shelves, frames, molding, bookcases, ladder, kitchenware, bucket, mast, telephone pole, railway ties, fences, splinters, gates, stairs, ships, toys, pencils, paper, matches.

EXERCISE 1—STAGE 3

TREE (species): birch, maple, beech, poplar, holly, sycamore, sumac, catalpa, alder, dogwood, ash, buttonwood, palm, willow, sequoia, oleander, yucca, mahogany, ebony.

TREE (fruit): apple, cherry, plum, pear, peach, apricot, orange, grapefruit, lemon, lime, banana.

TREE (nut): oak (acorn), chestnut, walnut, filbert, hazelnut, butternut, pecan, almond, coconut.

TREE (coniferous): spruce, pine, cedar, hemlock, fir, juniper, yew, larch, tamarack, deodar.

NOTE: Items italicized in Stage 1 suggest those of other stages: *bark* leads into *wood products*. It also suggests *birch,* a *species* of tree; so does *syrup,* representing *maple. Fruit* triggers a whole class of trees (as listed); *nut* does the same, while *cones* and *needles* suggest the *coniferous* or *evergreen* group listed.

□ GROUP ASSOCIATION KEY LIST □

EXERCISE 2—STAGE 1

HOUSE: arbor, abode, address, bower, bungalow, cabin, camp, castle, château, cot, cote, cottage, country seat, domicile, dwelling, farmhouse, grange, habitation, hermitage, *home,* homestead, hovel, hut, hutch, igloo, lean-to, lodge, manor, manse, mansion, palace, pagoda, pavilion, pergola, residence, retreat, shack, shanty, shooting box, shed, stable, tepee, tent, tower, townhouse, villa, wigwam.

EXERCISE 2—STAGE 2

HOME: attic, bay window, barn, basement, bathroom, bedroom, billiard room, bin, boudoir, bunker, cabinet, cellar, closet, chamber, conservatory, corridor, chimney, crypt, cupboard, den, doghouse, dinette, dining room, drawing room, dungeon, furnace room, fireside, gallery, garage, garret, greenhouse, hall, hearth, kitchen, kennel, laundry, lavatory, library, living room, lobby, loft, mezzanine, music room, master bedroom, nook, nursery, office, outhouse, pantry, parlor, passage, piazza, playroom, porch, portico, porte-cochère, roof, reception room, recesses, refectory, rumpus room, scullery, sewing room, sitting room, shed, sleeping porch, smoking room, stairway, steps, storage room, subcellar, vault, veranda, vestibule, walk, washroom, workshop.

□ GROUP ASSOCIATION KEY LIST □

EXERCISE 3—STEPS 1 AND 2
STREET: alley, artery, avenue, boardwalk, boulevard, bridle path, bypass, bypath, byroad, byway, battery, causeway, circle, coach road, concourse, court, crescent, crossroad, cut, detour, drive, esplanade, expressway, footpath, freeway, highway, lane, mews, pass, promenade, parkway, path, place, plaza, post road, quickway, right of way, road, roadway, route, strand, short cut, skyway, square, speedway, terrace, thoroughfare, thruway, towpath, track, trail, turnpike, viaduct, walk, way.

□ EXPANSION THROUGH CONTEMPLATION □

Having gone through the exercises given in the preceding pages, you are now ready to expand your findings through further contemplation. Taking the lists singly, read them over and analyze them as you go along. Note terms you should have included in your own list but didn't; also add any that occurred to you but were not in the printed list. Then take particular note of any with which you were unfamiliar; check them in a dictionary if you want to be sure of exactly what they are, though in some cases they will be self-explanatory.

Next, allow a time lapse of an hour or more while you put your mind to other matters. Or, if you prefer, you can go through all the lists, analyzing each in turn, so that when you go back to the first one it will be like starting all over, since it will no longer be fresh in mind. You are then ready for:

CONTEMPLATIVE REVIEW
This cannot properly be classed as an actual exercise because there is no special effort involved, but it gives good results. Simply repeat Group Association Exercise 1 through the steps already described, using the initial target word, *tree*, just as you did before. The difference is this: In the original exercise, you advanced from concentration to contemplation through the use of visual imagery that brought latent impressions from the unconscious to the conscious level. During this review, those impressions should still be at the conscious level, except for a few that may have slipped back. So now, instead of using associations to stir memory into action, you will be using memory to strengthen those same associations.

List them and compare with the originals; then make another contemplative review with Stages 2 and 3 of Exercise 1, listing each in turn. During these (particularly in Stage 2), you may find that new associations increase your list, which is possible if you expand its scope by going into deeper contemplation. Then go ahead with reviews of Exercises 2 and 3 on the same basis, listing them as well. Any additional exercises involving targets of your own choice should also be reviewed in this manner.

It is a good plan to repeat at least one of these reviews a few days later, to see how effectively the associations follow their original pattern, but there is no need to carry the process further. It is better to take new targets that will further reveal the vast scope of ideas that can be stored away and brought to light through contemplation. Such words as *bank,* with its checks, savings, personnel, and so forth; *hardware,* which covers dozens of items in daily use; *farm,* with all its crops and implements, are all highly provocative. Add to those *cities, states, countries, sports;* then go into subjects that interest you, such as *animal, bird, flower*—anything that is specific rather than general and offers prospects of a potentially large listing.

By the time you have gone through a dozen of these, you may find that you have close to a thousand things in mind you hardly realized were there, yet which are not only there but are also on call. With contemplation as your key you can unlock the strongbox and let those associations pour forth in an endless stream. *Bear in mind, however, that the purpose of these preliminary exercises is not to strengthen your associations but to multiply them—to enable you to realize through contemplation how far and how widely you can travel in the realm of the inner mind.*

Strengthening associations involves a combination of concentration and contemplation, thereby becoming an important adjunct toward memory development, which will be examined in Chapter 9. For the present, you are looking back on the seeds of thought that you planted in the unconscious through concentration and finding ways to harvest them through contemplation. That brings up another phase of the probe method which can be tested through the following exercises.

□ CHAIN ASSOCIATION □

BASIC EXERCISE
Start with a fairly simple word, but one that produces an immediate image. Rather than something that can be visualized in detail, with many ramifications, it should be quite limited, even to the point where you would have to strain to pile up close associations as in the group-association system. Since contemplation calls for relaxation, avoid all strain by steadily forming a single link to another idea and from that to another, using any idea or image that comes into mind.

Step One: Read the instructions carefully to get off to the right start; once you begin to move, you must stay on the track. Have paper and pencil handy, then pick a random word and repeat it aloud a few times, concentrating on that one word only, dismissing anything else from your mind.

Step Two: Do a simple time count up to thirty seconds, keeping the word in mind either as an image, a sound, some other sensory impression, or simply as an idea—even just a written word. If you have trouble doing this, dismiss the word from the mind, decide upon another, and start over.

Step Three: On completing the count, write the word on the pad. Concentrate on it or the image or sensation it induces and let that impression gradually fade. Relax, letting a new impression fill the void.

Step Four: Whatever the impression is, write a word to represent it just below the original word. Let the new image develop, then fade, to be supplanted by another image or idea.

Step Five: Write the new word below the other two and let it fade, so another can replace it as a new link. Write that down, let is link up with another word, and so on until you have listed six or more.

Step Six: Stop whenever you wish. Review the list and analyze it for further reference. Three types of stopping points are:
1. When you feel a satisfied sense of completion.
2. When a new impression fails to develop soon.
3. If there is conflict or confusion between new ideas. Decide on one and end it right there.

Having read the instructions, you are now ready to begin the exercise. Take the word *bell* as your starter. Compile your list; then turn to the end of the chapter and see how it compares with others that started with the same word.

ADDITIONAL EXERCISES

After analyzing your list, you can try the Chain Association Exercise again, patterning your procedure somewhat in relation to the results of your first try. If your chain reactions formed a smooth, somewhat spontaneous sequence, your best plan is to repeat the procedure, using another basic word. Some suggestions are *dawn, friend, party, peace, wave.*

If you were forced to hesitate or found yourself changing your mind regarding an impression somewhere in the chain, go back to that link as a starting point, do another count (Step 2), write the word again (or another in its place), and begin again from there (Step 3).

In reviewing the list, look for target words that would be suitable for a Group Association Exercise (pages 100 to 106). If you find one suitable for that purpose, use it in that type of exercise—provided, of course, that you have not already used it as a target in that type of exercise.

MUTUAL PARTICIPATION EXERCISES

You can turn mental exercises into fun and games, something I have both advocated and injected into my personal appearances in college auditoriums and on television. Just as people enjoy competitive physical activities, so can they profit through mental contests, as can be seen from the popularity of quiz shows and the like. But as a means of combining concentration with contemplation to the improvement of both, this takes on a new and greater aspect, which makes everybody happy.

With two or more participants, you can go through modified forms of Group Association Exercises and Chain Association Exercises as well. But instead of a *competitive* practice, this can become a *contemplative* process. Physical activity involves challenge, mental activity calls for cooperation. When two persons, each compiling similar lists, compare the items listed, it should prove of benefit to both.

The Alphabet Game is an old-time party pastime that covers this activity perfectly. You pick a broad subject— names of animals, birds, flowers, cities, countries, even makes of automobiles or general trade names. One player starts with the letter A and others do the same in rotation. Thus, with animals as a subject, such names as antelope, armadillo, anteater, and aardvark might be called in turn, with a player passing if he can't think of another A. When all pass, the next player names an animal beginning with B, such as bear, which could be followed by baboon, bighorn, beaver, and so on. This continues through the alphabet, finishing with Z, which is represented by such animals as zebra and zebu. Letters like Q and X can be skipped if no player can come up with a suitable name.

Games such as this lead to mental development, as do quizzes, crossword puzzles, word hunts—any form of fun or recreation in which you tap or utilize the latent knowledge your conscious mind has stored away in your unconscious.

The real secret of mind expansion lies in keeping the mind in balance through the methods and exercises described so far. We have seen how the conscious and the unconscious work in tandem; how imagery induces recall; how assimilation alternates with association; and how concentration and contemplation represent the ultimate in true mind development and its maintenance.

□ CHAIN ASSOCIATIONS □

Using the key word *bell* in the Basic Exercise, the following thought chains were formed by four different persons:

Bell	Bell	Bell	Bell
Church	Fire	School	Liberty
Sunday	Store	Bus	Bicentennial
Monday	Insurance	Airplane	Parade
Office	policy	Vacation	Horses
Lunch	Safe-deposit	Skiing	Racetrack
	box		
	Bank		

□ 8 □
UTILIZING THE MIND CONDITIONER

In your efforts to develop and expand the working of the inner mind, you have so far dealt with purely mental factors such as concentration, time counts, visual imagery, and other phases of expression relating to the inner self. These can be classed as experiments in awareness, because through them you become aware of certain built-in capabilities you probably did not realize you had; these in turn serve as steppingstones toward the attainment of many more.

Just as the conscious mind expresses itself in physical terms of seeing, hearing, talking, walking, and other everyday activities, so does the unconscious assert its own reactions. These include many things that are automatic or spontaneous, along with those that are classed as reflexes. But between the two is a vast borderland that includes vestiges of both, the only question often being which takes precedence.

Like the visible portion of an iceberg towering above the sea's surface, the conscious mind constantly observes, notes, and compares a multitude of things that go on about it. One great asset of a keen outer mind is its ability to dismiss things that are unimportant to one's main purpose. That nevertheless does not mean that such items have gone unobserved or unnoticed; quite the contrary. They are simply relegated to the unconscious, where the inner mind evaluates them according to its set of rules while the outer mind still works on what it originally regarded as the only matters worthy of prime consideration.

I say "originally regarded" because of that wide borderline between the two minds where there is often a question as to which should take precedence in certain matters. In fact, this is often dependent purely on personal opinion. You can test this for yourself by inviting three people of different tastes and inclinations to attend a party or visit some new place together. Afterward, their recollections or impressions will vary greatly, often to the point of dispute regarding some definite fact that can easily be proved if checked. Their opinions may be colored by what they thought they saw or wanted to see rather than what they did see.

But that is not all. Wait a few days and ask the same people to review their impressions of the event. Usually they have changed considerably. Why? Because the conscious mind has continued to dismiss certain things as unimportant, while the unconscious, still evaluating the doubtful data, has come up with items it regards as good enough to replace what the conscious has rejected. This ability to amend decisions and improve recollections while strengthening them represents a merging of the minds that should be cultivated to the full.

You don't have to wait to test other people with this process. You can apply it to yourself right now. You should be well equipped to do so if you have been practicing the exercises given so far, because they all are steps toward mind conditioning. Thus, in studying your own case along with others, you may swing to the rather startling conclusion that somehow your inner mind has observed and put away certain facts that escaped your outer mind entirely. Yet such can hardly be the case, for the conscious mind is obviously the observer of outside events and the unconscious merely the recipient. What can happen, though, is this: The conscious mind, continually feeding cast-off impressions to the unconscious, may often pass along items that the unconscious can match up with material it already has, coming up with an idea which seems entirely new when raised to the conscious level. This is an occurrence many people mistakenly term a "stroke of genius," never realizing that it is simply a function of the unconscious mind that can become quite common if properly encouraged.

How do you encourage the unconscious? By letting it act on its own, like the conscious mind. Many people, from the time they wake in the morning until they go to sleep at night, are under the continuous, all-compelling power of the conscious mind. One telephone call reminds them of others they ought to make; they then proceed to make them. One appointment leads to another, fulfilling a prearranged schedule. They dictate letters and listen to the playback of their own voices. They sign checks and cash them. They can drive through one red light, reminding themselves not to risk driving through the next one. By the time the day is over and they are turning on the television set, they might be lucky enough to spare a few minutes from their conscious life and dip down into the unconscious.

And what does the unconscious have to offer? Plenty. Our exercises in mind expansion and mental imagery have already shown that, but they have been based on cooperative effort. Either the outer mind must concentrate on some problem that only the inner mind can solve or the outer mind must clear itself completely to allow the inner mind to speak for itself. One way for the unconscious to speak its piece is through a device I call a mind conditioner. It consists of a weight suspended on the end of a thin string. A fishline weight is excellent if available, but a latchkey is more practical. By tying one end of the string through the hole in the

key, the string can be held so the key points straight
downward. A child's top, a rubber ball, or even a wad of
bubble gum may serve as a pendulum, as the device is
sometimes termed. But the ideal conditioner consists of a
small crystal ball less than one inch in diameter, permanently
affixed to a thin, flexible chain approximately eight inches
long.

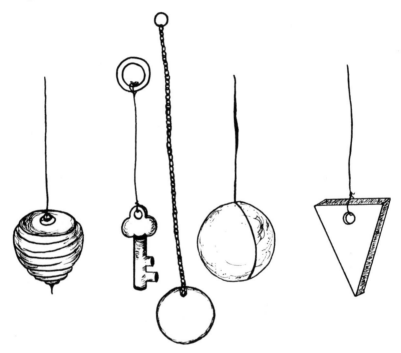

The ball, being a miniature crystal, enables you to concentrate upon it as it dangles, thus freeing your mind from
outside thoughts that might divert you from your main
purpose, which is to interpret the motion or behavior of the
crystal. The firmly set chain operates with precision, while its
flexibility enables it to respond to the impulses provided by
the unconscious just as readily as your everyday actions are
governed by the suggestions of your conscious mind.

When the upper end of the chain is held lightly between the thumb and forefinger with the ball dangling several inches below, the bob, as the pendulum is commonly called, will begin to swing back and forth. If you keep watching this motion, it will tend to increase as though you were exerting some control. If you mentally urge it to change its motion and move in circular fashion, it will tend to do so. We say "tend" because the result varies with different individuals. In some cases the change from oscillation (the original swing) to gyration (the rotary motion) does not take place until after several trials. In fact, some beginners become discouraged, thinking that they will not be able to make the pendulum gyrate at all.

Far from being a bad sign, this is a good one, for it proves that the beginner, overeager to make the pendulum gyrate, is applying conscious effort and therefore preventing the unconscious from providing the required impetus. With each repeated trial, the beginner should relax, letting his mind gradually change from "swing" to "rotation" until the pendulum responds. It is then that the device takes on the aspect of the mind conditioner that it will prove itself to be the more often you utilize it.

Some people claim that the change in motion is simply autosuggestion, which is true to a certain degree, because autosuggestion can stem from the unconscious as well as from the conscious mind, and sometimes more readily. In fact, a primary function of the mind conditioner as a device is to enable the inner and outer minds to function on a cooperative basis. A beginner who finally gets the bob to gyrate often finds it a slow process and therefore strains consciously in order to speed the result. Such effort may become painfully noticeable, both by observers and the operator.

There are two quick ways to cure this problem once you have found that you can make the changeover, even though the bob may be slow in its response. Let it start its usual sway as it dangles from your right hand, but instead of becoming tense and wishing it would rotate, simply bring your left hand just beneath it. Altmost immediately the bob will switch from oscillation to gyration, in some cases so rapidly that you wouldn't have had time to will it, either consciously or unconsciously. This really shakes the skeptics who claim that the muscular action of your right hand is responsible for the pendulum's motion, because it is your left hand that influences the changeover without even touching either the chain or the bob!

The other method of accomplishing the same result is to get the bob oscillating nicely and take a deep breath while you watch it. Hold your breath for several seconds, then exhale in a long, continuous fashion. Gyration will result in the same surprising fashion. Even doubters, induced to try one of these methods for themselves, will find that the same thing happens for them, proving that the conditioner is a "convincer" in its own right.

You are now ready for the conditioning exercises that follow. A good preliminary test is to lay a ruler crosswise on a table and hold the conditioner so the bob dangles over the very center.

Concentrate on the ruler as a target and watch the bob swing back and forth, staying along that fixed line as though the ruler were exerting a magnetic force. Even if you shift your hand to different spots along the ruler, the swing will continue, often increasing its length. One important thing about this test is that it detaches your thoughts entirely from the pendulum, thus putting the unconscious in full control. True, you are watching pendulum's action, but it seems fully impelled by an outside source.

That in turn injects another potent factor: the direction of the pendulum's swing. Hitherto it was somewhat unpredictable. With some operators, the tendency would be to oscillate from left to right or crosswise; with others, it might go to and fro or inward and outward. The same person may find that the pendulum swings crosswise one time, outward or even at an odd angle at another. Any of this can give an operator some feeling of personal control, which he loses when he takes the ruler as his target.

When you reach the end of the ruler, another surprise may be in store. The swinging stops and the bob begins to gyrate, with the end of the ruler as a focal point. Here again, the action approaches the automatic since you have taken a new target. Carry the bob all the way to the other end of the ruler and it will gyrate there as well, but in the opposite direction. (At least, that is how it works with some persons, though it may vary with many others.) If you come approximately close to these results, you should proceed directly to:

□ THE MIND-CONDITIONER EXERCISES □

For these, you need the special chart illustrated on page 122. Copy it exactly on a sheet of paper about seven inches square. It shows two crossed lines of about two and one-half inches in length, one bearing the word *yes* at each end, the other the word *no*. These lines serve as your oscillatory targets, the circle as your gyratory target.

All your preliminary experimentation with the conditioner will prove valuable now, because you should be loosened up to the point where the device can practically take over on its own, letting you follow its lead. You should be able to test the conditioner without the slightest conscious effort on your part; if not, relax and revert to some of the earlier stages before concentrating on the chart, which will be your guide from here on. Your focal point is the crossing of the two lines, the *yes* line being vertical (away from you), while the *no* line is horizontal (running from left to right).

Hold the conditioner so that the bob dangles a few inches

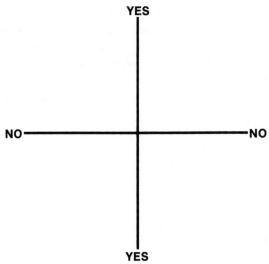

above the focal point and consciously ask a simple, direct question to which the answer is obviously yes so that the unconscious can respond by activating the bob accordingly. A very natural question would be: "Am I now ready to test the mind conditioner?" Even as that thought comes to mind, the pendulum may begin its forward and backward action, sometimes almost anticipating the question. Even if the response is slow, it can be regarded as satisfactory provided no conscious effort is involved. In any case, you then stop the pendulum by lowering the chain so that the bob touches the focal point. When the bob is lifted it will simply wobble erratically and will be ready to respond to the next mental direction.

For some people, the pendulum springs a surprise on its first trial by swinging crosswise instead of lengthwise, thus responding with no instead of yes. If it does the same when tried again, turn the chart so the *yes* line is horizontal and the *no* line is vertical. Extensive experimentation has shown that the conditioner works that way in some cases.

In any event, the conditioner should be double-tested by

stopping the pendulum again and testing it with some "no" questions, which should also be the obvious sort. In this position, if the pendulum swung vertically for yes, it should now swing horizontally for no, but in cases where the chart had to be turned so the *yes* line was crosswise, you will invariably find that the *no* line should be lengthwise, so the problem automatically takes care of itself, giving further evidence that the unconscious is responsible.

After the *yes* and *no* lines have been tested satisfactorily, poise the pendulum anew and concentrate on the circle. Now your conscious question should be one that can definitely be answered "I don't know"; as you think of it, the pendulum will automatically begin to gyrate, with the circle as its target, widening its range as it continues. Usually the motion is clockwise (to the right), but with some people it will circle counterclockwise, possibly because the person is left-handed. This possibility should also be tested with further questions to make sure of the individual's predilection. Choice of suitable questions is highly important during this test, as the unconscious can be highly exacting in its interpretation of a conscious question and if in doubt as to the answer may spin the pendulum the wrong direction.

As an example: If the weather happens to be threatening and you ask your inner self "Will it rain today?" you would expect the pendulum to rotate clockwise, saying "I don't know," which is true enough. But the question could indicate some special interest—even concern—on your part with regard to the weather that your unconscious did not share. Thus by reversing the pendulum's rotation, the inner mind could either reject the question or tell the outer mind "I don't care." Any such ambiguous questions or answers can be avoided when testing the conditioner with a group of people by having each person call his question out loud for all to hear and check. A question such as "Does Janet have blond hair?" would call for an appropriate yes or no if Janet happened to be there for all to see; the answer to "Is today Wednesday?" would be equally self-evident.

Another advantage of testing with a group is that many people are encouraged to try the conditioner for themselves after witnessing the trials made by others. This simplifies the procedure without in any way detracting from the results, and often the enthusiasm expands as more people get into the act. In contrast, there is always the chance of striking a snag if you suddenly precipitate a person into a conditioner test without any preliminary briefing. The presence of other people as witnesses can create an unconscious reaction in complete opposition to normal expectations.

I encountered such a situation when I was called upon to explain and demonstrate the working of the mind conditioner before a group interested in its scientific possibilities as a parapsychological instrument. Far from being skeptical, they had been impressed by reports about it. So I held off all preliminaries until the key member of the group arrived. He showed such immediate interest when I brought out the pendulum and the chart that I saw what I thought was a perfect opportunity to let the mind conditioner practically speak for itself. I placed the chart squarely in front of him, put the chain in his hand, telling him just where to hold it, and had him poise the bob over the spot where the lines crossed. With that, I told him, "Now, think of any question that you would like answered by one word: yes."

As I spoke, I sensed the question that was forming in his mind. It was simply "Will this gadget work?" That was indeed a perfect question. His eyes were fixed so intently on the bob that even the slightest sway would be an affirmative indication, and I hoped to see the pendulum gaining its customary motion in a slow but steady style. I couldn't have asked for anything better, but what actually happened couldn't have been worse.

The pendulum hung stock-still!

That was something I had never seen happen before and have never seen happen since. Invariably, the pendulum will move slightly in an erratic manner even though there is no conscious effort on the operator's part. At times further motion may be delayed or the pendulum may behave in faltering fashion while the unconscious is gradually taking control. But here the situation was an absolute blank. As tense moments passed, the case became more critical. I had stated that the pendulum would act, and unless it did I might as well forget it. To halt the test would be an admission of failure; it would be even worse to let someone else try it and have it work, for then the key man would be totally convinced that it would never work for him.

Groping for a reason why he had so completely frozen, it suddenly occurred to me that his conscious mind had focused entirely on the pendulum instead of the word *yes,* which he had unquestionably uttered unconsciously. The only remedy was to reverse that situation. On impulse, I extended the tip of my forefinger beneath the motionless bob; then, being seated directly opposite the man, I drew my finger slowly toward myself along the *yes* line, to the very end.

The effect was electric. From a standing start, the bob swung outward as though magnetized. Inward—outward— inward—outward: the pendulum action was increasing with each swing. The operator's eyes were following it and so were those of all the onlookers. When I asked what the man's question was, he told us: "I wanted the gadget to show us if it worked—and it did!"

It continued to work for him and the others who were present; in fact, in terms of group results, it was perhaps the best demonstration of the mind conditioner's reactions I have ever witnessed. But what was even more impressive was its proof of the power of the unconscious, as I analyzed it afterward. It came to this:

Anyone who sincerely seeks to gain real results from the

mind conditioner will naturally try to aid its action consciously during the preliminary exercises and early trials. As you become aware of this, your trend is to counteract that impulse by consciously retarding the pendulum's action. As these trends balance each other, some other factor must necessarily assume control—the unconscious.

In the case just described, the operator, being a man of solid judgment, began by trying to retard the pendulum consciously instead of seeking to help it. That impulse was so fixed that when he consciously reversed it, he could not get far enough beyond the balance point to force the pendulum to move. By believing it was impossible, he made it impossible. Either way, autosuggestion provides the keynote. People who insist that anything is possible usually are forced to admit that such a belief may have its limitations; but the same applies to persons who claim that something is impossible.

The value of the chart in early tests is that it diverts the conscious mind from its seesaw practice of helping and hindering the pendulum, by getting the conscious mind to concentrate upon the lines of yes and no or the circle that signifies "I don't know" or "I don't care." So when I saw that the operator's conscious mind was frozen on the pendulum, I released it by drawing attention to the chart, so that *his* unconscious could take over, which it did.

These points will be further emphasized in the exercises that follow.

□ 9 □

EXERCISES WITH
THE MIND
CONDITIONER

The exercises so far given with the mind conditioner are largely preliminary, enabling you to familiarize yourself with the device and thereby appreciate its possibilities. That does not mean that they should be discarded once you have moved on to the more advanced exercises in this chapter. You should revert constantly to the basics, not only to refresh yourself on what you have already learned but also to reach the point at which handling the pendulum becomes spontaneous.

Compare yourself to an artist who thinks in terms of pictures and lets his hand draw them; or a musician who lets the melody flow from his mind into the instrument his fingers are playing; or even the typist, who knows that the letters Q, W, E, R, T are at the upper left of the keyboard but can't remember their order beyond that, yet can read from a book and automatically transcribe its wordage into correctly typed pages.

Treat the mind conditioner in that light and you will be amazed by the results it brings. Until you have reached that point, you should have the pendulum handy, or even carry it with you, in order to tap the resources of your inner mind whenever occasion offers. Dr. Leslie LeCron, of Los Angeles, a famous clinical psychologist, carried a pendulum with him all his life because he gained such good results from it. You, too, can gain results beyond all expectation by maintaining your basics while you move into more advanced exercises.

FIRST EXERCISE: CONCENTRATION

Simple though this is, it represents the keynote for all that follows. It must be practiced regularly, not just occasionally, to insure responses that are both spontaneous and register a true expression of the inner self.

Step One: Choose a time when you can focus your mind directly on the conditioner, giving it your full attention for a period of at least *five minutes.* In addition, *plan ahead* by choosing a time when you can *repeat* this practice session at regular intervals under similar conditions. These should be scheduled at least *once a day* in order to gain the desired result, which is to detach your conscious mind from the action until it becomes virtually automatic.

Step Two: Dangle the pendulum freely at the length you find most suitable, resting your elbow on the table if your hand is at all shaky or your arm becomes tired. Use of the chart is optional, particularly in the early stages, but as you continue you may find it preferable to do without it, since you already have it fixed in mind.

Step Three: Think in terms of yes until the pendulum follows that line; then stop it with your other hand and repeat the process with no. Another stop and you can follow with the circular motion of "I don't know"; then do the same with the opposite circle for "I don't care." If you wish, you can count the seconds during this procedure.

Step Four: Repeat the four basic response movements of the pendulum. As a variation, you can concentrate on having it slow down and stop, although it is probably most effective if you simply lower the pendulum so that the base touches bottom, stopping it voluntarily. As it stops, you can think in terms of the next action, letting the pendulum go from one into the other. As you continue these sessions, you can add new variations to the action of the pendulum.

Not only does this exercise help to speed up the earlier modes of concentration with which you are already familiar, it can also create a favorable attitude for further concentration as well as the advanced exercises that follow. Most important, it gives you confidence in your ability to use the pendulum to a degree that will convince skeptics.

SECOND EXERCISE: CONTEMPLATION

Now you move into the second phase of mind development, with which you already are familiar. Once more the conditioner can intensify the process and supply impulses of its own, all aiding you to attain a contemplative mood.

Step One: Concentrate on causing the pendulum to swing *horizontally.* This time you are not seeking a negative answer but a *receptive mood.*

NOTE: Even if your reactions are reversed, with yes representing the horizontal instead of no, you still should concentrate on a horizontal swing. As the swing begins, gaze intently into the pendulum itself, as if to fix in mind what you see there.

Step Two: Let this induce a relaxing impression of a basic sort. For most people *color* is the ideal thought, which they have gained through earlier practice in contemplation. Green, blue, brown, and other colors may come to mind in whatever shade you find most helpful. For some, *shapes* furnish relaxation: clouds, trees, hills, or even geometric figures (a square, a circle, a triangle).

Step Three: Repeat the phrase "peace and calm" ten times, keeping count with the fingers of your left hand so as not to distract your mind from the repeated phrase. At the finish, lay the pendulum aside, rest both hands on the table or in your lap, and close your eyes. Immediately:

Step Four: Take five deep breaths and relax with your eyes still closed. Let your mind drift; don't try to keep it blank. If you actually visualize a color of which you have been thinking, so much the better. The same applies to other thought impressions; and if you feel detached from reality, maintain that inner mood until your mind gradually returns to its surroundings. Then count one to five and open your eyes. (This technique will not only assist you in schoolwork but will aid as well in studying any material you wish to learn.)

Perform all these actions calmly and deliberately, particularly when opening your eyes, since the purpose of this exercise is to draw impressions from the inner mind and retain them.

THIRD EXERCISE: PREPARING FOR STUDY

This requires a combination of concentration and contemplation, hence you must program yourself at least two weeks *in advance* to fulfill the requirements of the study technique. These preliminary steps are included in the routine.

Step One: For one week, practice the concentration technique in Exercise 1 for five minutes a day. In addition, repeat this procedure for a minute or more at the end of each day, preferably just before retiring, to assure that the technique is functioning properly.*

Step Two: During the second week, practice the contemplation technique on the same basis: five minutes daily, with the brief checkup later. Note that each technique is being conditioned *in turn.* Do not alternate them in these preliminary practice sessions.* That comes with:

Step Three: At the start of the third week, gather all your books, notes, references, and other material. Dangle the pendulum in readiness for concentration and when it swings in a circle, say with your lips: "I am becoming deeply engrossed and absorbed in my studies." If the pendulum stops circling and responds with a yes, lay it aside and proceed with your studies. Otherwise:

Step Four: Repeat the statement after a few moments, giving the pendulum another chance to respond. You can repeat this three more times if necessary, making five times in all. If the pendulum does not finally respond with a yes, postpone your studies until later.*

FOURTH EXERCISE: COMPLETING STUDIES

Assuming that all has gone well during your preparation for study and that you have actually begun a period of study, you can move from a stage of concentration into contemplation. Check the time at which you began and proceed as follows:

Step One: After a period of about half an hour, stop studying and return to the pendulum. Hold it in the usual fashion and concentrate on having it swing in a circle. When it does, speak with your lips as you did before, this time saying: "The material I have studied will come to me whenever I want it."

Step Two: Do not wait for the pendulum to stop. Let it continue to circle while you repeat the new statement five

---

* If at any time the pendulum fails to respond or you feel too tired or sleepy to continue, wait until later to continue, even if that means until another day.

times at regular intervals. The circling motion will gradually swing into a continuous yes (up and down), signifying that your conscious statement is registering itself in your unconscious mind.

Step Three: Lay the pendulum aside and take a break of five to ten minutes, casually thinking back to the facts you have just studied. That done, you are ready to begin all over again, combining Exercises 3 and 4 into one unit.

THE COMBINED EXERCISES

Step One: Start the pendulum circling and repeat your original statement ("I am becoming deeply engrossed and absorbed in my studies") until the pendulum again responds with a yes. Lay it aside and resume your studies.

Step Two: At the end of half an hour, again stop studying, pick up the pendulum, and concentrate on the circular action. When the pendulum responds, repeat five times over: "The material I have studied will come to me whenever I want it."

Step Three: Lay the pendulum aside, but this time do not merely take a break. Instead, review the material with the feeling that you have completed your studies. During the review compare the results with those you gained during your early break. You will be surprised how readily you now recall the material.

☐ 10 ☐

MEMORY
Applying It to
Mental Discipline

In our study of the inner mind along with its development and control through recommended exercises, I have emphasized the three Cs of concentration, contemplation, and coordination. With CONCENTRATION, the power of *suggestion* comes strongly to the fore, setting the pattern of all that follows. With CONTEMPLATION, the law of *association* manifests itself to a remarkable degree. Through COORDINATION, the faculty of *recall* exerts itself, enabling the inner mind to assume full control, tapping the vast reservoir known as memory.

This concept, which has been demonstrated in the preceding chapters, is at variance with the current misconception advanced by many memory "experts." They treat memory primarily as a function of the conscious mind, a faculty that can be strengthened like a muscle, through constant exercise of a physical sort. Though they recognize that the unconscious plays a definite part, they minimize it so much that it loses its real impact. Using the analogy of the mind as an iceberg, they concern themselves with the visible tenth above the water's surface rather than the nine-tenths below. Or, if we consider memory as something like petroleum, they are content to get their supply from a gasoline pump instead of drilling an oil well.

It is true that most modern memory systems use association as their basis. This is nothing new. Such methods date back to the ancient Greeks and Romans, who used the "link" or "chain" system. But today's "experts" have strived to outdo the ancients through the creation of artificial devices—some very ingenious—many of which make it easier to remember the memory links than what you were using the links to remember.

□ ATTENTION + INTEREST + REPETITION = AIR □

Step outdoors on a beautiful spring morning. Its tang will command your *attention*. That arouses your *interest,* so you take a few deep breaths to inhale the fragrance. They are so good, you keep on taking more. That is *repetition*. The capital letters of those three key words spell AIR, the vital factor in everybody's life. You will always remember a day like that, and you will want to live it over because it will be fixed in your unconscious as a standard of comparison. Multiply that by a vast variety of other experiences—good, bad, or indifferent—and you will realize the important part that the AIR formula plays in shaping your memory.

Actually, the AIR system works in rotation. You don't have to start with attention to trigger it. Interest in some activity can cause you to repeat it and thereby capture your attention; that is how new fads get started. Similarly, constant repetition of anything can force you to give it your attention and thereby rouse your interest—the secret behind advertising jingles that drill themselves into the public mind. Whether you spell it AIR, IRA, or RAI, the formula still works. As philosopher Charles Fort observed: "One measures a circle beginning anywhere."

The simplest and probably most primitive of memory devices is that of using the forefinger of one hand to count the thumb and fingers of the other. The ancient Romans derived their numerals from that procedure. The thumb was raised as I on the count of one, the forefinger as II, for two, the next finger as III for three, the next as IIII for four, while the thumb and little finger were spread with the others doubled in between to represent V for five. Later, the count of IIII was lessened to IV, representing "one before five" or four. A switch of hands enabled the counter to go on with VI for six, VII for seven, VIII for eight, IX for nine, and X—as a double V—for ten.

This type of memory tab is still in use today and any criticism of it as a childish practice is unjustified because the roots of memory begin early and form a nucleus for much of the expansion that follows. In checking a limited number of items (say, up to a dozen) it's natural to use the finger count, repeating it with the same hand after reaching five instead of switching hands as the Romans reportedly did. Thus you can count off the seven days of the week in regular order; the same applies to the twelve months of the year.

In both instances, the process is extremely useful, as you may suddenly want to know how many days it is from this Wednesday to next Monday, so you begin your count on Thursday and end on Monday, making five in all. Similarly, with the months, you don't have to remember them by their numerical position so that you can date a letter 7/23 to represent July twenty-third. Just use the finger count, starting with January, and you will hit July on the count of seven.

At this point you can inject a supplementary device to take care of an ever-present problem. Everyone knows that the long months of the calendar have thirty-one days and the short months thirty, with February having only twenty-eight, plus an extra day in leap year. Remembering February's status is no problem, but many people have trouble recalling which are the "long" months and which the other "short" ones. All you need to set this straight is to shift your monthly count from tips of thumb and fingers to the *knuckles* of the fingers and the *spaces* between them. Thus the right forefinger would begin its count on the knuckle of the left forefinger, proceeding as follows:

Knuckle of left forefinger:	January
Space between next finger:	February
Knuckle of left second finger:	March
Space between next finger:	April
Knuckle of left third finger:	May
Space between next finger:	June
Knuckle of left little finger:	July
Knuckle of left forefinger:	August
Space between next finger:	September
Knuckle of left second finger:	October
Space between next finger:	November
Knuckle of left third finger:	December

Each knuckle represents a month of thirty-one days; each space a month of thirty days or less, which makes it easy to identify the "longs" and "shorts." After counting the knuckle of the left little finger (July), you automatically return to the knuckle of the left forefinger (August).

Quite as important as numbers are the letters of the alphabet and the order in which they appear—essential for looking up words in a dictionary or names in a telephone book. Occasionally letters function as numbers; for example, the fourteenth row in a theater or stadium would be Row N. They can be counted on the fingers in groups of ten: A through J, first ten; K through T, second ten; with the last six letters, U through Z, as an additional group. Many memory jogs are dependent on familiarity with the alphabet, as will be seen in certain systems that follow.

Figures, days, months, and letters of the alphabet and their order are all learned through repetition (by rote) at an early age. Many other things can be committed to memory in the same fashion, including the names of friends, places, and so on. Notes of the scale, multiplication tables, colors of the rainbow, and many other items may also be learned readily by rote, hence it was a common type of instruction during the days of limited education. Its chief fault is that unless you keep repeating the data thus committed to memory, they will gradually fade from lack of use.

That is where association comes into play, through the formation of memory links that spring automatically to mind, thus doubling one's vocabulary at the very start: great and small, better or worse, ham and eggs, over and under, meat and potatoes, cats and dogs are common examples of such linkage. These have also been forged into such triple links as man, woman, and child; good, bad, and indifferent; pants, coat, and vest. Many trade names and slogans have been based on double or triple linkage, for instance Currier & Ives and Stop, Look, and Listen.

In these two examples, visual imagery becomes an added function. Currier & Ives were the makers of lithographs depicting early American scenes, so any mention of their joint name will bring such pictures to mind. Similarly, STOP, LOOK, AND LISTEN was the warning sign at railroad crossings, so that slogan conjures up memories of locomotives, freight trains, and even wrecks. Put that imagery in reverse and any reference to early American will make you think of Currier & Ives while any talk about railroads may wind up with somebody repeating "Stop, look, and listen!"

Various devices can be used for linking facts as well as names. As a starter, try linking the names of some states with their capital cities. There are two that are immediately obvious: The capital of Oklahoma is Oklahoma City; the capital of Indiana is Indianapolis, which means the same thing. Now let's look for lesser links that can be applied in other cases.

The capital of New York is Albany. The abbreviation for New York is N.Y. The name of Albany ends in NY. Think of it as AlbaNY—or AlbaNY, N.Y.

The capital of Vermont is Montpelier. Vermont is known as the "Green Mountain State" represented by the word *mont* (*Ver* = the French *vert,* green). The last syllable of the state name is the first syllable of the capital: VerMONT— MONTpelier.

The capital of Kansas is Topeka. The last two letters of Topeka form the beginning of the name Kansas. TopeKA— KANsas.

The capital of Maryland is Annapolis. Think of Mary's full name as Mary Anna. *Mary's land* is *Anna's city:* MARYland— ANNApolis.

The capital of Maine is Augusta. Maine is known as "Vacationland." Think of people taking vacations in *August* and going to *Maine*—Augusta, Maine.

The capital of Alaska is Juneau. In June the weather gets warmer in Alaska, so: In *June, you* should go to *Alaska*— Juneau, Alaska.

Other links of states and capitals are possible, such as the name Providence, capital of Rhode Island, containing the initials of the state: pRovIdence. Unless you find that such links come easily, it is better not to overstrain them. This is also true for other types of paired names.

The association of names through their initial letters is a very effective device for remembering a specific list. These too are made to fit the situation and therefore take varied forms. Here are some good examples:

BAHAMAS—BARBADOS—BERMUDA

These groups of islands once had the same type of government under the British Colonial system. To remember the islands' names, people referred to them as "The Three Bees."

Bahamas
Barbados
Bermuda

THE SOLAR SYSTEM

Here is a memory link used to remember the planets of the solar system in their exact order moving outward from the sun. List them in a column at the left; at the right, form a column from a coined sentence, using the same initial letters for each succeeding word:

PLANETS	INITIALS	SENTENCE
Mercury	M	Men
Venus	V	Very
Earth	E	Easily
Mars	M	Make
Asteroids	A	All
Jupiter	J	Jobs
Saturn	S	Serve
Uranus	U	Useful
Neptune	N	Needs
Pluto	P	Pleasantly

Assume that you have given the list of planets your *attention;* then added *interest* in facts pertaining to them. Your problem is *repetition,* particularly in their order from the sun outward. So you switch over to the silly sentence and memorize it by repetition, because it means nothing else than "Men very easily make all jobs serve useful needs pleasantly," which is a lot easier than remembering the names of the planets in their established order.

So time goes by. You think about the planets and recall everything except their exact locations. Then you remember that "Men very easily make all jobs serve useful needs pleasantly," and by counting the capital letters twice over on your fingertips you come up with Mercury, Venus, Earth, Mars, Asteroids, Jupiter, Saturn, Neptune, Uranus, Pluto.

That's great if you are interested in traveling to outer space, but suppose you would rather remain on earth and settle in some simple place like Central America. That could mean going into the banana business, which is somewhat overworked, or trying your hand at coffee, which might have big future in those countries. So line them up, from north to south, in the column on the left, and express your hopes in one sentence on the right:

COUNTRIES	INITIALS	SENTENCE
Belize	B	Banana
Guatemala	G	Growers
Honduras	H	Help
El Salvador	E	Establish
Nicaragua	N	New
Costa Rica	C	Coffee
Panama	P	Plantations

Just seven countries to remember, which is quite simple, particularly if you study a map to start; but to put them in their proper order and keep them there can be a problem since you have passed the stages of *attention* and *interest,* leaving only *repetition*—which may bog down if neglected. So new AIR with the key sentence produces the same capital letters as the needed link.

You can make up sentences of your own to fit the names of friends or places you are anxious to remember and reel off in regular order. The more appropriate the better, but even farfetched links will stand up if repeated fairly regularly. However, much tighter links can be formed through the use of acrostics, in which the capital letters spell a key word of their own. Here are some excellent examples:

POINTS OF COMPASS

North
East
West
South

Think of NEWS coming from all directions.

BRITISH ISLES

Wales
Ireland
Scotland
England

Picture WISE men in each nation.

GREAT LAKES

Huron
Ontario
Michigan
Erie
Superior

Picture HOMES built around the Great Lakes.

SOUTHERN EUROPE

Portugal
Albania
Yugoslavia
France
Italy
Greece
Spain

Think of people giving their PAY for FIGS.

Remembering each key word or phrase along with the items forming the list makes it a fixed adjunct and an ideal link. It is frequently difficult to form good keys, otherwise this device would be more commonly used; nevertheless this technique has led to the coining of self-descriptive terms that have increased our modern vocabularies. Here are some examples:

Alnico—An alloy of aluminum, nickel, cobalt
Amtrak—American railroad passenger service
ASCAP—American Society of Composers, Authors, and Publishers
AGVA—American Guild of Variety Artists
Boatel—A hotel for boat owners
Brunch—Combination of breakfast and lunch
Calexico—A California town on the Mexican border
Conrail—Consolidated Railroad lines
Delmarva—The Delaware–Maryland–Virginia peninsula
ESP—Extra-Sensory Perception
Frigidaire—A make of electric refrigerator
Interpol—International Police

Lucite—A transparent plastic
Mexicali—A Mexican city on the California border
Motel—A hotel for motorists
Nabisco—A special product of National Biscuit Company
Necco wafer—Product of New England Candy Company
PTA—Parent-Teachers Association
RSVP—Please reply (French: *Repondez s'il vous plâit*)
Smog—A mixture of smoke and fog
Texarkana—Town on Texas–Arkansas line
TV—Television
Uneeda—Trade name of a biscuit (*You need a* biscuit)
UN—United Nations
Univac—Universal Automatic Computer

Linking words by mental imagery can be carried to perfection where the signs of the zodiac are concerned. With astrology a subject of general interest, many people would like to call them off like the calendar months, but remembering the signs in their regular order may pose a problem. Here is the way to solve it. You start with the sign of Aries, the Ram, on March 21, and list the remaining signs as beginning about the twenty-first of each succeeding month. Then set your sights on this picture story:

Think of a RAM (Aries) boldly attacking a big BULL.
The BULL (Taurus) goes wild and chases two TWINS.
The TWINS (Gemini) stumble into a pool and a big CRAB emerges.
The CRAB (Cancer) uses its claw to grab the tail of a LION.
The LION (Leo) wakes up and gives a roar, scaring a MAIDEN.
The MAIDEN (Virgo) runs away and drops a SCALE she is carrying.
The SCALE (Libra) hits the ground and rouses a SCORPION.
The SCORPION (Scorpio) stings the heel of an ARCHER.
The ARCHER (Sagittarius) shoots wide, just missing a GOAT.
The GOAT (Capricorn) becomes excited and butts a WATERMAN.
The WATERMAN (Aquarius) upsets his jar and out pour some FISH.
The FISH (Pisces) scatter widely and are noticed by the RAM.

By now you should be sufficiently familiar with the link system to use it as a basis for visual imagery that will enable you to remember just about anything. The ancient Romans called this the place system, because they picked a familiar house or grounds and moved from place to place within it. You can do the same today with your house, apartment, office building, shopping center, or a ride downtown. For a standard pattern, let's suppose that you are Mr. X, who owns a simple suburban home and that you are arriving there right now. Picture yourself proceeding as follows:

1. You drive your car into a GARAGE in the basement of the house and leave it there. You go

2. Into your WORKSHOP, look around for a few moments, and proceed up the steps

3. Into the KITCHEN, where everything is spick and span. There you turn to the right

4. And enter the DINING ROOM, where the table is all nicely set for a meal. Another turn

5. Brings you into the LIVING ROOM, where you warm your hands at the fireplace and

6. Look out through the door to the enclosed FRONT PORCH, as you start upstairs, where

7. The master BEDROOM is situated on the left. Directly in back of that

8. Is the BATHROOM and across the hall from that, you glance into

9. The PLAYROOM, where toys are scattered on the floor. From there you go forward

10. Into the GUEST ROOM at the front of the second floor.

Now assume that you, as Mr. X, have the following things to do: (1) Mail a registered letter. (2) Leave a watch to be repaired. (3) Buy some shaving cream. (4) Stop to pick up a friend. (5) Deposit some checks at the bank. (6) Attend a service-club luncheon. (7) Buy some tickets to the circus. (8) Bring home candy for Mrs. X. (9) Phone friends about meeting them for dinner. (10) If they say yes, get dressed for dinner; otherwise, forget it.

So you start your day in reverse. You think of driving home into (1) Your *garage,* where the door is barred and the post office clerk is registering your *letter.* That done, you think of (2) your *workshop,* where you are trying to fix your *watch,* but can't, so you keep it for the jeweler and go into (3) the *kitchen,* where all you can find in the refrigerator is *shaving cream.* You move on to (4) the *dining room,* where your *friend* is waiting to have a cup of coffee. From there you enter (5) the *living room,* where you toss a bundle of *checks* into the fireplace and look out to (6) the *porch,* where all the members of the *service club* are waiting for you to join them. So you go upstairs to (7) the *bedroom,* where you find *elephants* (and other circus animals) in full control. Therefore you put the candy in (8) the *bathtub* and cross over to (9) the *playroom,* where you pick up a toy *telephone* and call your friends, so they can decide if you go into (10) the *guest room* and get *dressed for dinner* or just *stay home.*

You can extend this list by picturing: (11) an upstairs hallway, (12) a finished attic, (13) an attic storeroom, (14) the roof above, and (15) a chimney.

You can also use the list over and over, because each time you list a new sequence of things to do, you will automatically eradicate the old one, just like rubbing out chalk writing on a blackboard. If you want to retain a list for a long time, don't disturb it. Choose another setting as your key—a neighbor's house or apartment, a suite of offices, the stores forming a shopping center, or simply such furniture and other objects around a large living room as (1) bookcase, (2) sofa, (3) coffee table, (4) chair, (5) desk, (6) doorway, (7) telephone table, (8) window, (9) television set, (10) radiator.

The secret of this system is that its links are things with which you are *familiar,* usually in the form of *places.* Thus it can really live up to the claim of *instant memory,* because you start *immediately* with something *already known,* which is a *permanent* fixture in your mind. To each link of the chain you hook something *unfamiliar, unknown,* and often *temporary.* The linkage demands *attention* to start; it takes *interest* to form and visualize the links; and if you run through the finished chain several times, *repetition* will clinch it, again proving the effectiveness of the AIR formula.

People who have tried this system at my suggestion have been so surprised by their own ability that they have frequently exclaimed, "Why, it's as simple as ABC!" That puts them right in line for the Alphabet System, which begins with A–B–C and keeps right on through X–Y–Z. In learning the alphabet, children are frequently given words to represent each letter, along with an appropriate picture, so it is quite natural to apply that process to the Alphabet System, linking the words as well and using a few more sophisticated terms than those found in childish lists.

ALPHABETICAL KEY LIST

APPLE, falling from a tree covered with
BULBS of varied colors, like a Christmas tree, with a
CAT sitting beneath, looking warily at a
DOG, which is starting to bark at an
ESKIMO who is looking in amazement at a bed of
FLOWERS which are growing just outside a
GATE where a driveway leads up to a small
HOUSE that is nestled at the foot of a large
ICEBERG. On the summit you see a
JUGGLER, who suddenly starts flying a large
KITE, which disgorges a large batch of
LETTERS that come fluttering to earth, where a
MONKEY grabs them but can't read them, so gathers
NUTS from a tree and throws them down to an
OCTOPUS, who drops them into a large
PIGGY BANK that is officially presented to a

QUEEN seated on a throne at the bow of a
ROWBOAT, where the scene shifts to a
SAILOR pulling at the oars and looking at a
TURTLE who swims to shore and takes shelter under an
UMBRELLA, where you see an oversized
VASE being balanced on the pointed nose of a
WALRUS, who is keeping time to a
XYLOPHONE being played by a bearded
YOGI seated on the back of a
ZEBRA, who can be easily identified by his stripes.

Of course, this list is arbitrary and you can use any other objects you prefer, provided that you keep them in alphabetical order. The "story line" is a help toward remembering the list exactly as given, but after using it a while you won't really need it. Your key words will simply be:

1. APPLE	11. KITE	21. UMBRELLA
2. BULB	12. LETTER	22. VASE
3. CAT	13. MONKEY	23. WALRUS
4. DOG	14. NUT	24. XYLOPHONE
5. ESKIMO	15. OCTOPUS	25. YOGI
6. FLOWER	16. PIGGY BANK	26. ZEBRA
7. GATE	17. QUEEN	
8. HOUSE	18. ROWBOAT	
9. ICEBERG	19. SAILOR	
10. JUGGLER	20. TURTLE	

This gives you a complete list of twenty-six keys which for convenience are divided into two groups of ten each and an extra group of six. To remember the list of ten things given earlier, you could use this A–B–C system as follows:

1. Picture an APPLE resting on a REGISTERED LETTER.
2. Think of BULBS on a tree with your WATCH hanging there.
3. Picture a CAT all lathered up with SHAVING CREAM.
4. Think of a DOG biting the FRIEND you are to pick up.

5. Picture an ESKIMO depositing CHECKS at a bank.
6. Think of a FLOWER in everybody's buttonhole at LUNCH.
7. Picture yourself going through a GATE to the CIRCUS.
8. Imagine a miniature HOUSE made entirely of CANDY.
9. Visualize yourself on an ICEBERG making a PHONE call.
10. Imagine a JUGGLER tossing your best CLOTHES in air.

For more items, you would simply go on from there, utilizing the key list up to as many as twenty-six, which is more than you would normally need to go. But you are by no means limited to that total, for you can readily prepare an alphabetical list of your own to take care of another twenty-six. Reference to a dictionary can help you in such choices, and even the letters X, Y, Z are no great hazard: X offers X-RAY and XEROX, with such terms as EXIT or EXPERT being quite allowable; Y provides YAK, YACHT, YAM, and YEOMAN; while under Z you will find ZEBU, ZITHER, ZOUAVE, and ZIGGURAT. Reverting back to Q—a fairly hard letter—you have choice of QUAGGA, QUAKER, QUILL, and QUINCE, plus others.

What raises the A–B–C system to the peak of perfection is the fact that, since it is alphabetical, it can be used to remember *numbers* as well as *words*. In this case no linkage of objects is needed. Just think of key pictures in terms of figures from 1 to 9, adding 0 instead of 10. Visualize those figures somewhat as follows:

For 1, picture a large single object to conform with your alphabetical list. Thus you would think of a BIG APPLE or a BIG HOUSE. For 2, visualize a pair, perhaps TWO ICEBERGS floating side by side. For 3, think of a TRIANGLE, as three kites flying in triangular formation. For 4, picture a SQUARE, as four cats, each in a corner. For 5 either a PENTAGON or STAR formation. For 6, various formations will do, as SIX MONKEYS forming a pyramid, SIX XYLOPHONES in groups of three each, or a ZEBRA with six alternating stripes. For 7, you can think of the object as LUCKY. For 8, visualize objects in a DOUBLE SQUARE or in a SOLID GROUP, like a bed of flowers, a block of houses, or a squad of sailors. For 9, make it a MULTITUDE, with a field of flowers, enough houses for a town, enough sailors for a ship's crew. For 0, make the thing a BLANK or OBLITERATE it. An ICEBERG would be melting; a ROWBOAT would sink; a ZEBRA would run away. You'll be surprised how easily you can form these negative impressions.

Play around with those impressions and then get down to business. Suppose you want to remember the number 2152582957. How would you do it? Easily! Using the A–B–C system, you picture

A PAIR of APPLES, side by side.	(2)
A BIG electric BULB, like a searchlight.	(1)
FIVE CATS forming a basketball team.	(5)
TWO DOGS on leashes, going opposite ways.	(2)
FIVE ESKIMOS, forming another basketball team.	(5)
A COMPLETE BED OF FLOWERS, nicely arranged.	(8)
A PAIR OF GATES, so take your choice.	(2)
You are in town, with HOUSES all around.	(9)
And ICEBERGS in star formation, closing in	(5)
To say: "Look at the LUCKY JUGGLER do his act."	(7)

Read that over, run through it by the A–B–C system and you won't forget it. I know, that's the way I remembered it. It happens to be a *telephone number,* which breaks down into 215-258-2957 and which is very important to me. If you want to remember another phone number, switch from your first set of keys, A to J (APPLE to JUGGLER), to the second set, K to T (KITE to TURTLE). For another, go to the third set, U to Z (UMBRELLA to ZEBRA), reverting to A, B, C, D to add four more, such as ARTIST, BALLOON, CLOUD, DUCK.

With phone numbers, you seldom need the first three figures representing the area code and usually you only need to remember such numbers temporarily, otherwise you would keep a written list of them. Thus you can use the same list over, by mentally wiping out old phone numbers, street addresses, zip codes, and the like in order to remember new ones. With important phone numbers or items like Social Security numbers, you can keep them *permanent* if you *personalize* them. Picture the person whose number is involved as being part of the scene and being in the midst of any action it suggests; as eating *apples,* putting *bulbs* in sockets, petting *cats,* and so on.

That way, you will have it pegged, but if you have to keep a lot of numbers constantly in mind, it is better to have special lists so there will be no confusion with the standard list that you use regularly for temporary purposes. Here is a good list—broken into groups of ten—that is easy to fix in mind: all the keys are items found around a kitchen. It is given in plurals since the list is intended for remembering numbers only:

APRICOTS, BUNS, CUPS, DISHES, EGGS, FORKS, GLASSES, HOT-CAKES, ICECUBES, JARS . . . KNIVES, LEMONS, MUSTARD, NAP-KINS, ORANGES, PICKLES, QUINCES, RADISHES, SPOONS, TURNIPS . . . UNEEDA (crackers), VEGETABLES, WAFFLES, OX-HEARTS (cherries), ZUCCHINIS, AVOCADOS, BANANAS, COCONUTS, DATES.

From the practical standpoint, the A–B–C system represents the limit to which most persons should go in the field of memory improvement, because they can get immediate results with the first ten letters of the alphabet and then develop it further to suit themselves or their own requirements. Those who like it and find uses for it will find that the system grows of its own accord because it involves natural associations they can shape in whatever way they want. The tendency among memory "experts," however, has been to play down this all-purpose method and go into artificial formulas or phonetic systems that require the memorizing of one hundred limited words based on an arbitrary arrangement of such consonants as T, N, M, R, L, SH, K, V, P, and S or their equivalents, with the vowels A, E, I, O, and U serving as fillers along with the letters W, H, and Y.

The last three letters, incidentally, spell *why*—and that is what you ask yourself once you embark on such a project, because familiarizing yourself with its basic rules is almost like learning a new language—and to make it all the more complex, the experts have vied with one another to run the list up to a thousand such key words. All are phonetic, so if you forget any of them, you can form your own as you go along, but that can prove difficult with your choice limited to certain consonants that must be arranged in a specific order. I have never met anyone who uses the phonetic system except memory experts themselves, probably because it takes so much time and effort to become proficient in this method that they have to go into the business to make it worth while.

Like the A–B–C system, phonetics and other trick methods do help you to use your imagination, but where alphabetical links form natural links and are easy to picture, the complex systems require associations that are farfetched and frequently outrageous. This also applies to tricky systems of remembering people's names by using words or phrases that sound something like them. Quite a few of these are close to insults, so care must be taken in using them, like thinking of Hogarth as Hogwash, Fitchett as Fidget, Stangler as Strangler, or Holden as Hoodlum; while others form odd pictures, like Stuyvesant as Tie-vest-pants, Houlihan as Hole-in-one, or Callahan as Call-a-hand. But these are makeshifts, often used by memory experts to call off names of persons present at some function.

There is only one way for people to remember the names of persons they really want to know and therefore want to remember. That is to apply the AIR formula to its full degree. Any time you meet anybody, give that person your full *attention*. You do that for one good reason: You expect the other person to give you all of his or her attention, which makes it *reciprocative*. This is something you won't find in most memory systems: *reciprocation*.

You tell people who you are and what you do. They listen. They tell you who they are and what they do. You listen. That is *attention*. You ask them more about themselves, their families, their friends. That is *interest*. So they ask about you, your family, your friends. Afterward, you repeat to yourself what they told you. That is *repetition*. They repeat what you told them. Or will they?

There are several answers to that question; of that you are sure. You *do;* maybe *they don't.* Either way, you can't lose. If you *do* and they *do,* you meet again on mutual terms: Each recognizes the other. If you *do* and they *don't,* all is in your favor. If you *don't* and they *do,* you should be ready with apologies. If you *don't* and they *don't,* you can both begin all over.

You can insure that result through *multiple associations*. Don't be satisfied with what people tell you about themselves; ask them to tell you more. The more they do, the more you will impress them and the more links you will establish. Often you will find that you have a mutual interest; if not, the very lack of one can prove to be a link. Points of conflict also serve as memory jogs. In applying the AIR formula to remembering names, the emphasis should be on the letter I, which in this case stands for "individual" as well as "interest."

Don't forget yourself, where the letter I is concerned, either. The more closely you can identify your purposes with those of people you want to remember, the stronger the links will become. If you find that you have mutual friends, that will prove a help; if not, try to think of old friends your new acquaintance would probably like to meet or who would like to meet him. Whether they actually meet or not, they will be associated in your mind, thus adding another memory link.

By using multiple association, the quickie method of

remembering names temporarily, such as thinking Harryman for Harriman or Low-rents for Lawrence, can be put on a more permanent basis. You meet a man named Chichester; instead of linking him with the uncomplimentary term "Shyster," you keep thinking of his real name, Chichester, while you talk with him about things that interest him. In so doing, you find that his favorite game is chess, so immediately you think of Chichester as "Chess Master," which he may indeed be.

□ 11 □

GAINING
SELF-CONFIDENCE
THROUGH MENTAL
DISCIPLINE

All the exercises and methods so far detailed in this volume are pointed toward a single purpose: namely, to develop your capacity for mental discipline to such a degree that it can be applied with positive results in your daily life. You have learned how the power of the inner mind can solve dilemmas, enable you to make decisions, and bring your latent faculties, including memory, into constant use. In this and subsequent chapters, we shall see how specific techniques can be used to deal with typical problems affecting us all.

As a basis, we can refer back to Emile Coué, the French pharmacist who became a psychotherapist and popularized the slogan "Every day in every way, I am getting better and better," which a few million Europeans and Americans began chanting with such regularity that many of them began feeling better and better.

My own formula for a relaxation conditioning exercise is based on *"Kreskin's conditioning is becoming deeply entrenched in my unconscious,"* which is easy to remember and becomes a frank statement of an actual fact the longer you use it. It is used as an adjunct to any of the conditioning exercises given in previous chapters and the procedure is as follows:

Step One: Each night for two weeks, assume a comfortable position conducive to sleep, close your eyes, and repeat the phrase exactly as given, moving your lips without actually vocalizing.

Step Two: Continue to repeat the phrase slowly, in the same mental fashion, keeping count by pressing downward with the fingers, starting with the left little finger as one and running to the left thumb as five; then from the right thumb as six to the right little finger as ten.

Step Three: Repeat the phrase in the same manner, running from ten to twenty, left to right. Let your fingers count *automatically* while you repeat the phrase *mentally*, letting your lips express it *silently*. All this is *important*.

Step Four: After finishing the second finger count, reaching the total of twenty, let your mind drift. *Do not doze off before you finish the automatic count.* By then, you will have reached the state of relaxation that you seek.

After following this procedure for at least two weeks, you will have a tendency to fall asleep in the middle of the finger count. This is quite all right because the habit pattern will have become so effectively entrenched in your unconscious it will still tend to finish to the twentieth repetition, your lips moving and your fingers counting even while you are in the lighter levels of sleep.

Note that this procedure is the direct opposite of Coué's formula, which was designed to start off the day with a pepped-up outlook—which too often could wear off as the day progressed. In fact, a "Let's go!" attitude can produce tension instead of eliminating it, whereas my overnight method enables you to pick up and start a few steps ahead of where you left off the night before. All you need then is to be ready for any obstacles that may block your path. In short, having gained relaxation unconsciously, you must be able not only to renew it consciously but in some cases turn it into almost immediate action. This can be done through an exercise that will phase out all types of self-consciousness:

KRESKIN'S CONFIDENCE BUILDER

This technique, once mastered, can be applied to any personal situation. Since you have already programmed yourself through various exercises culminating in those that engender relaxation, you are ready to take this step beyond, which will produce direct results in overcoming stage fright or selling your ideas to a skeptical client, with a whole range of situations in between.

In a real sense, you are now familiar with the method about to be described; it is a blend of the countdown system given earlier and the relaxation process just described, plus sidelights derived from other familiar sources. First I shall describe the general procedure, then cite case histories and examples of its application under specific circumstances.

Step One: After a few weeks of conditioning from concentration through contemplation and finally into relaxation, adopt the slogan: *"I can relax more and more easily whenever and wherever I desire. I can relax more and more easily whenever and wherever I desire."* Repeat this several times until it becomes almost automatic. Then:

Step Two: Write the statement word for word on a sheet of paper, or close your eyes and imagine that you are writing it. (Writing is preferable in most cases, but if you have developed a high degree of visual imagery, you can probably picture the words as vividly as if they were written.) Now read the words slowly, repeating them emphatically to yourself, and fold the paper. Or imagine yourself going through that procedure.

Step Three: Now close your eyes, take five deep breaths, and hold the fifth as you mentally spell R–E–L–A–X slowly and emphatically. Exhale and keep your thoughts blank so that words from the slogan such as *whenever* or *easily* or *relax* or *desire* slip in and out of your mind. This process will become effortless, with each random word serving as a key to the whole statement.

Step Four: Continue this *without counting,* simply letting habit decide when you reach the zero mark. By that stage, the word *relax* should be sufficiently predominant for you to resume spelling it R–E–L–A–X, with each letter serving instead of a word in completing the countdown. Then:

Step Five: As you mentally intone the letters R–E–L–A–, emphasize the final X and immediately *reverse* the others: A–L–E–R–, adding a final T. Repeat this—A–L–E–R–T—then pronounce the entire word: *Alert!*

This can jolt you from relaxation into realization, for the simple reason that emphasis on the word *relax* gradually relieves all feeling of pressure, so that the switch to *alert* produces a desire for challenge, a readiness to meet any issue that may confront you. Taking these in logical order, we have:

☐ STAGE FRIGHT ☐

In my work, demonstrating the power of suggestion, stage fright became a challenge from the very start. I soon learned that in order to meet it head-on, I had to dismiss all thoughts of failure from my mind. That is how I learned to turn relaxation into realization and also why I developed the confidence-building technique just described.

Before facing an audience, I went through the Relax–Alert routine until it became second nature, so that now I can snap into the climax instantly. For anyone whose work holds a similar challenge, I recommend the same procedure as a sure safeguard against stage fright.

Lecturers can conquer stage fright and turn the tide their way. Their system is to set their sights on a sure-fire anecdote or clever saying that will win people to their way of thinking. They hold this in reserve for fifteen minutes. No matter how badly the affair starts—people are slow in coming in, the chairman makes too long an introduction, the microphone won't work, or the lights go off—the lecturer can count on the fact that when the time comes he or she will take control; the worse it was before, the better it will be if the lecturer practices the confidence-building technique.

THE REHEARSAL TECHNIQUE

In contrast to comedians and lecturers, who can remain themselves before an audience, an actor must play a part in which he assumes a personality distinct from his own, even one he doesn't like. (Sometimes a hero role is worse from the actor's standpoint than playing a villain, because it may mean that he has to live up to something beyond his normal capacity.) Stage fright during a performance may result in anything from missing an important cue to forgetting lines entirely; in either case, it can bring disaster upon not only the actor but the entire show.

One way to prevent this is to rehearse a part to the point of absolute perfection, but that in itself is a problem. A few days before the opening of a show, an actor may get the recurrent feeling that he needs "just one more rehearsal" before he goes on. After that rehearsal, he will want another—and another—until he may be confronted by the fear that he has had too many and has "gone stale" in the part. He may feel lost just before the curtain rises on the actual show, and full-fledged stage fright can take over.

Such a crisis must be met in the usual way—by applying the Relax–Alert routine exactly as described above. But even if this gets you off to the right start, there is always the chance that as the show progresses the old qualms may return. Something must be done to counteract the problem, and that is where the rehearsal technique comes in. It works like this: From the moment you feel the symptoms of stage fright creeping over you, switch to the attitude that you don't have to do the show at all instead of tensing yourself with the grim thought that "The show must go on." Instead, right now, tell yourself that you can forget the audience and go through another rehearsal.

If you felt that you needed just one more, this will be it. Conversely, if you think you overdid it, you know the part so well that you can play around with it, adding the neat touches you may have neglected because your mind was so fixed on making every detail letter-perfect. Either way, backtrack to that last rehearsal, picturing yourself strengthening it or lightening it. Actors who have used this method have told me that they lost all dread of critical audience reaction because they didn't realize that an audience was out there until they had gotten completely past the crucial stage.

PROJECTING TO THE FUTURE

Here is another method of mental discipline that I devised to meet a special emergency and have since recommended to many people with good results. I was called upon to help a young but highly talented opera soprano prepare for an audition that, if successful, would give her an immediate role with the Metropolitan Opera company. The score was both complicated and elaborate, which worried her greatly because she felt that listeners would be judging her in terms of flaws or mistakes rather than recognizing the true quality of her voice and delivery. This had me worried, too, for I saw the logic of her argument and realized that the tension it induced would mar her natural ability to the point where failure would be a certainty.

I gave her a cram course in relaxation and self-confidence. That would have solved almost any other problem, but when we got back to the matter of the audition, she choked as badly as ever. The rehearsal technique bogged down completely, because the audition itself was in one sense a rehearsal—in fact, that was its big trouble. Then, suddenly I thought of the solution: to put the process into reverse. Instead of backtracking to the rehearsal stage to help minimize the strain of working before a critical audience, why not project ahead and meet the challenge of an imaginary audience to relieve the pressure of the actual audition!

It worked like a charm. This budding star had often pictured herself singing at the Met. Now she would be realizing that ambition, for the audition was the equivalent of a minor role in an opera. Each time she went through the aria, she eliminated all thoughts of the audition committee and—instead of going blank when she reached the intricate parts—she gave them her very best as she visualized a packed opera house with the applause echoing from every quarter.

She passed the audition with flying colors and went on to a highly successful career, with never a vestige of stage fright; the bigger the audiences, the more they reminded her of her first triumph, the audition she dreaded so intensely. Her case can be applied to many other phases of life where the challenge of the future can outweigh the pressure of the present. Part of the key to the common malady of stage fright is to use the imagination to desensitize yourself gradually. Imagine yourself in front of a group that is fairly small but large enough to make you apprehensive. Imagine yourself performing the activity or recital you intend. Run it over and over in your mind, gradually imagining yourself feeling at home in front of such an audience. On the next practice session increase the size of your audience and rehearse mentally your rendition with that group until you picture yourself at ease and confident.

□ APPLYING THE RELAX–ALERT □
FORMULA IN VARIOUS DEGREES

You don't have to be a professional performer in order to build self-confidence through the methods just described. Stage fright actually is far more common in everday life than on the stage or lecture platform or in the audition room. Most people just don't recognize it. Once you regard yourself as a Very Important Person, you will realize how strongly this applies to *you*.

Put yourself in *the place* of the lecturer, actor, or singer and you should be impressed by your *immediate gain*. Suppose you are asked to head a civic committee and give a plaque to some local notable. You foolishly accept the assignment and find that you must impress people with *YOUR* importance to start; otherwise you wouldn't be up there on the platform where you suddenly wish you weren't. The only solution is to be *yourself*. You can do that by first schooling yourself in Kreskin's conditioning program, then coming through with Kreskin's confidence-builder just before you have to deliver the plaque.

Will it be worth it? Yes. From then on you will be called to deliver bigger things in a bigger way, until you become so good that you will not only like it but will be able to knock down any remnants of reluctance by repeating the Kreskin formula when needed.

You may be drawn into some local theatricals by playing a part in a benefit show; or you may be asked to deliver the main speech for an important occasion, introduce a speaker, or dedicate a cornerstone. You will be in the position of an actor, who has to project the "person" he wants the audience to see, as we have discussed in establishing the rehearsal technique.

Use the future projection technique to the full. You don't have to be an opera singer to apply it. Whether you are teaching Cub Scouts how to tie knots or telling jokes at a local clambake or giving a talk before hundreds of people, you can assure success through this technique.

□ 12 □

APPLYING MENTAL DISCIPLINE TO ATHLETICS

Sports present various complexities that can only be unlocked through concentration, visual imagery, contemplation, and other keys to inner-mind expansion detailed in preceding chapters.

In athletics the inner mind must supply a degree of coordination along with constant attention, even with the simplest of exercises, such as skipping rope. These, in turn, lead to more exacting pastimes that require participants to develop further functions of the inner mind.

Here are some examples:

Paul Pesthy, an outstanding Olympic fencer, uses the time between matches to reduce the tension of the previous match. "You must be able to stop thinking of the last match," he reported. His method is to retreat under a blanket or towel, close his eyes, and imagine that he is drawing a large circle. He places the number 10 inside the circle. Then he draws a smaller circle inside the first circle, moves the 10 into the new circle, and adds a 9 outside the outer circle. Next he draws another circle inside the last one, moves the 10 into the new circle, transfers the 9 to where the 10 was, and adds an 8 inside the outer circle. This is a very demanding sequence, as if he were building a dart board in the most difficult way possible. This serves his purpose of shifting his attention from the previous match and focusing it on a neutral activity.

At the Winter Olympics at Innsbruck, Austria, in February 1976, Lyle Nelson of the United States performed brilliantly in the biathlom, an event that is not very well known in the United States. It combines the endurance needed in cross-country skiing with the precision of rifle marksmanship and is normally dominated by teams from Russia and Finland.

Nelson used psychological training to prepare himself beforehand.

Neil Glenesk is another famous Olympic athlete. In preparing himself for a series of fencing matches, he sits alone with his head down, his eyes closed, and mentally builds aggression and a feeling of hatred for the next opponent.

Austrian ski jumpers are sent to an institute for willpower training. Jean-Claude Killy, a three-time winner of Olympic gold medals, has said that his only preparation for one race was to ski it in his mind. He could only practice mentally, because he was recovering from an injury and could not appear on the slopes. That race turned out to be one of his best.

It is important that when the athlete—whether golfer, weightlifter, or tennis player—rehearses his sport mentally he should feel the muscles in action in his mind. Similarly, the musician—whether violinist or pianist, cellist, or trumpeter—should practice the same way when he is on an airplane or sitting quietly in a chair: by imagining that he hears the correct tones and the correct sounds and rhythms and imagine that he is making them. He will have an input of practice that will affect his actual performance.

This imagining and visualization of motor response— physical activities—results in more than pure imagination; it

is a well-controlled copy of experience, like a powerful
dream at night that one seems to be living through. '

Among the most popular of participating sports pastimes in
America today is the form of bowling originally called
Tenpins, to distinguish it from earlier versions of the game. A
player bowls a heavy ball down a long alley toward a group of
ten wooden pins set up in pyramid formation at the far end.
If he knocks them all down, he is credited with a strike; if
some remain standing, he is allowed to bowl a second ball in
hope of knocking off the remaining pins for a spare; that
ends his turn. A strike earns him 10 points, plus whatever he
makes on his next two rolls; for a spare he gets 10 points plus
his next roll; otherwise, he simply scores the total of his two
rolls, which may be anything from 0 to 9.

There is a story of a young man who was fairly good at
tennis, baseball, and basketball but had never bowled. He
went with some friends to a bowling alley and, seeing how
simple the game seemed, he decided to try it himself. He
weighed a ball, gripped it as the regular bowlers did, and
rolled it cleanly down the center of the alley, knocking over
all the pins for a perfect "ten strike." He waited eagerly until
the pins were set up again; then he went after another strike,
adding just enough more power to make sure he would clear
the pins again. To his amazement, the ball skidded along the
edge of the alley, flopped into the gutter, and floundered on
past the pins, missing them all. What seemed so easy had just
been luck, the kind that didn't repeat.

The man in question later became an excellent
bowler—and never forgot those first two rolls of his career.
All he had to do was shut his eyes and he could see them, one
after the other, and feel the double surprise he had gotten

long ago. When you begin to master its technique, bowling becomes a matter of visual imagery as well as physical exactitude; it is by synchronizing those two factors that some experts have managed to attain the goal of a "perfect 300" game.

Once you have become an ardent bowler, you will find it easy to picture yourself rolling strike after strike down your favorite alley. But try to turn it into reality when you get there! You are likely to become overeager trying to live up to your expectations, instead of letting your own skill set the pace while you picture yourself catching up to it.

One good way to start is to view yourself about to roll the tenth or final frame in a game where you need to make a strike in order to gain a bonus of two more rolls for a possible total of 30 points, enough to win. Shut your eyes with that in mind as you step up to the alley to bowl your first frame; then let go. If you score a strike, your mental imagery has proven its worth; if not, you still have a whole game ahead of you.

Some players follow the roll like a greyhound chasing a rabbit, gesturing toward the course they want the ball to take, wiggling their hands as they pray for a reluctant pin to topple. I have known others to shut their eyes before the ball is halfway down the alley so they can imagine it hitting the headpin while they listen for the crash that will indicate they have made a strike. Both types of bowlers are wrong. They are ruining their power of visual imagery at a time when it can't possibly do them any good. If they miss the strike, they will be deflated when they pick up the second ball and may well miss the spare to boot.

The thing to do is watch the ball's course so you can copy your roll exactly if it makes a strike. If it misses, you can decide whether you should have given it a bit more steam or perhaps eliminated some of the old force. Then forget it while you are picking up the second ball and inject a brief countdown, ending R–E–L–A–X—A–L–E–R–T! Then study the pins that are still standing and revert to visual imagery to picture yourself knocking them off for a spare.

Whatever happens, simply take it as a matter of course and get ready to visualize yourself making a strike on your next turn, correcting whatever mistake you made before. If you follow that procedure frame by frame, you may be more than surprised by the way you improve your score.

☐ HOW NOT TO BEAT YOURSELF ☐
ON THE GOLF LINKS

Compared to a bowling alley, a golf course is a tremendously big place; the action varies to a marked degree with every stroke and the intervals are long and far apart. All those are reasons the mind-conditioning techniques should differ with the two games; this is particularly true for visual imagery. In golf, there is one all-important rule toward improving your game through mind power. It can be summed up simply as "Never look back."

That may come as a surprise to the average golfer. All during the long trip out to the links and later, while waiting for his turn to start, the golfer is thinking of himself as a heroic figure, driving from the first tee; then adding his score at the first green and making another fine drive from the second tee, with a low score for the second hole; then driving in fine style from the third tee—and so on, as far as his imagination happens to carry him before he actually gets under way at the course.

Generally, he will skip ahead to round out this fantasy by bragging about his low score in the locker room and possibly celebrating the occasion by treating his fellow golfers to a round of drinks. For, whatever his ambition, this is the day he intends to attain it—whether he hopes to break a hundred, is good enough to finish in the high eighties, or is even so good that he might make it in a few strokes under par.

All this is looking ahead, not back. Now, suppose he does get off a good drive from the first tee and follows it with a good iron shot, a nice approach, and two good putts. All very fine, so far, but if he flubs his drive from the second tee and takes too many strokes for that hole, his calculations will be upset. In his eagerness to make up for the bad drive, he may overdrive the green on the short third hole and land in a sand trap that can cost him a few more strokes. From then on, the average golfer will generally decide that he would have done better if he had stayed home, now that bad luck has spoiled his day.

Actually, he spoiled it for himself, by giving himself a schedule he couldn't meet without having to look back on mistakes he couldn't rectify. Even if he hadn't indulged in that fanciful preview, he would be just as badly off if he started from scratch but kept thinking back to each hole while walking from a green to the next tee. That can be the death march to a golfer's hopes for two reasons: (1) If he worries over a bad hole, he will overstrain on the next, and (2) If he had a good hole, his jubilation can cause a letdown. The secret is to take each hole as it comes, considering it stroke by stroke, dismissing each hole from the mind as soon as its score has been marked.

You can do this by clearing your mind, using the hole you have just finished as a fading picture instead of a melting snowman (which would be out of character on a golf course). Let the count fade as you mentally slip into the spelling of R–E–L–A–X—R–E–L–A–X instead of numbers, and when you near the next tee reverse it to A–L–E–R–T! If your companions are talking along the way, give them a few nods but don't pay much attention to what they say. If they are talking about the last hole, don't give them any attention at all; you want to forget it, good or bad.

You will then be able to tee off like a master, even though

your drive may not attain that standard, and you can give the same attention to each succeeding stroke, keeping your cool when you reach the putting green. To prove this, just watch a few tournaments on television and see how the players' minds are geared to the immediate action. Statistics also bear this out. While writing this book, I took time out to watch a famous golfer gradually close a gap until all he needed was a par five to tie for the title. He reached the edge of the green in two—which meant that if he could run a long putt just short of the pin, he could hole out with a birdie four and win. Instead, he sank the long putt for an eagle three, clinching the match instantly.

There is nothing to stop you from pausing at a juncture like that and undertoning "I can relax more and more easily whenever and wherever I desire." You'll notice that a real pro always appears relaxed in such a situation. But always remember to add "Relax—Alert!" just before you make your putt.

□ CONTROLLING THE TIME ELEMENT □
BY CONCENTRATED RELAXATION

We now come to a comparatively lesser sport, that of skeet or trap-shooting, in which clay pigeons are hurled into air mechanically so that waiting marksmen may fire at them with shotguns. I am giving this in detail because of an important bearing it has on more active sports as well. In trap-shooting, the marksman must keep a steady vigil until the clay pigeon suddenly spins into sight; then he must follow through with quick action as he aims and fires at the moving target.

The shift from one mood to the other has an impact that catches many shooters entirely off guard. While watching, the time drags so slowly that they become impatient and the pigeon's speed confuses them. One keen observer, noting this, decided to gear his tempo to the long wait by relaxing and letting time drift by, confident that over-all action would be the same. What happened amazed him. Each pigeon seemed to "come up like a balloon" and he followed it with a leisurely aim that just couldn't miss. When he told this to other shooters, they wouldn't believe it until they tried it; then they had the same experience.

At the time, this discovery received the endorsement of a well-known sporting magazine; and for all those who want to try it, the Relax—Alert technique can serve beautifully. Simply keep repeating mentally "Relax—relax—" until time goes slower; then as the pigeon appears and your aim seems to come up slowly with it, the word *Alert!* will spring to mind at the right moment to fire.

That raises the question: Can time actually be slowed, making each moment longer to the human mind? Slow-motion movies have simulated this, but these come under the head of an optical illusion, produced by retarding the film so that each successive picture stays on the screen longer than normal. Yet there is a way of lengthening moments mentally through the aid of another type of optical device—a pair of field glasses or binoculars:

Using the glasses, station yourself where you can see some automobiles coming toward you at an angle along a road. As you lift the glasses and focus them to view a car's approach more closely, you will find that it seemingly slackens speed. Of course the car is magnified and therefore the distance is proportionately lessened, but the reduction of speed is definitely apparent. Another phenomenon, more in the nature of an actual illusion, can be noted by watching the big signs mounted above certain service stations to advertise their gasoline. These revolve at an even speed, but as they come endwise toward the onlooker they apparently move more rapidly, only to slacken as the broad side swings in view.

Such observations suggest mind-conditioning exercises that are applicable to those sports described in the next chapter.

☐ 13 ☐
MENTAL DISCIPLINE IN COMPETITIVE SPORTS

The gap between individual sports and those of a highly competitive nature involving team play is by no means so great as most people suppose. There are two ways to bridge the breach: One is by raising individual effort to a competitive level, the other is by concentrating on the part you must personally fulfill during team play. The basic techniques differ widely. In the preceding chapter we saw that visual imagery of the relaxation type is all-important in such activities as bowling, golf, and skeet-shooting. In the sports to be discussed here, the factors of instant recall and mental projection stand out. At the same time they involve visual imagery and imagination, so results gained from one field will apply to others.

☐ TENNIS AS A COMPETITIVE MIND CONDITIONER ☐

Like bowling and golf, tennis began as a simple and rather casual diversion and developed into a highly skilled sport.

Tennis was of much later origin and its evolution was therefore far more rapid—in fact, sudden. Originally called lawn tennis, the game was played on a court 79 feet long by 27 feet wide, crossed by a 3-foot-high net. Using wooden rackets strung with catgut, two opposing players hit a ball back and forth across the net, each scoring a point when one missed or hit the ball out of bounds or into the net.

For years the ball was lobbed back and forth in friendly style until clay courts supplanted grass to give the ball more bounce. Within a few years, the championship matches were dominated by "Big Bill" Tilden, whose powerful drives and return strokes overwhelmed all opposition. From then on, tennis became a high-powered, high-strung game that demanded not only physical conditioning but mind conditioning as well. Instead of simply putting the ball in action and picking up the play from there, the serve became the predominating factor. You should therefore give service first consideration whenever using mind conditioning to improve your tennis game.

In learning to serve, a player takes a designated position at one end of the court with a racket in one hand, a ball in the other. His situation resembles that of a bowler gripping a ball preparing to bowl it, or a golfer taking his stance and wangling his club back and forth before driving from a tee. In tennis, the server may decide upon his exact position, bounce the ball a few times, or even mop his brow before tossing the ball and swinging his racket to deliver the serve, so superficially the situation resembles bowling or golf. Actually, it is quite different, because the tennis server has *two factors* to consider: himself and his opponent. In bowling, he concentrates on the pins; in golf, he keeps his eye on the ball, confident that precise action on his part can produce a ten strike or a fine drive. But in tennis, perfect placement of a serve in an adversary's inner court is only half the struggle. It would score a point if nobody were there to prevent it, but with a competent opponent not only waiting for it but expecting it and therefore prepared to counteract it, you are faced by a double mental hazard.

In tennis, the server must control his action and at the same time allow for the receiver's reaction. That calls for an advanced type of mind conditioning to assure inner or self-centered control.

COMBINING MENTAL DISCIPLINE AND VISUAL IMAGERY

Picture yourself as a capable tennis player, sure of your ability up to a certain point. You have practiced serving until you have it down pat and you are about to deliver the first serve in the first game of the first set in an important match. Just as in bowling or in golf, you are ready to relax and then alert yourself to the test, knowing you should do as well as ever and perhaps even better. That is when you make the mistake of stopping to consider your opponent.

Let's take bowling as our best analogy, because in bowling you roll a first ball with the privilege of rolling a second if necessary; in tennis, if you miss with your first serve, it is termed a fault and you are given another try. In bowling, you play it "strong" by going for a strike on your first roll; if you miss, you play it "neat" by going for a spare on your second roll.

In tennis, they did pretty much the same back in the early days. If a player missed with his first serve, he took far more care with his second rather than risk a double fault, which would mean a lost point. But instead of winning a point by a powerful, well-placed serve, a player who practically lobbed his second ball over the net to make sure it landed in the inner court was playing squarely into the hands of an opponent who was not only waiting for it and expecting it but was prepared to make the most of it with a powerful return stroke.

In short, if the old-time server didn't massacre his opponent on the first try, he virtually offered himself as a victim on the second. All this because he magnified his opponent's potential and thereby lost confidence in his own. Present-day players frequently do the same to a marked degree if they make the mistake of concentrating first upon the serve, then adding the opponent as an artificial hazard.

You can spot a server of that type by the way he keeps fidgeting or talking to himself as he gets ready for the serve and then comes up for a mighty effort, taking in his opponent with a sweeping gaze as though intending to blast him right out of the court along with the serve that follows. One reason he can't is because he tries to put so much power on the serve that he misses the inner court entirely. Then, on the second try, you will see him planning a sure placement, talking to himself and finally giving his opponent some quick, apprehensive glances while he goes into the serve. Chances are that the opponent will rifle a return shot that will catch the server as off guard as a sitting duck.

All this can be overcome by the following procedure:

Step One: Study the situation briefly in preparation for your serve, then concentrate on your opponent's position in the court, adjusting your target accordingly. Then, instead of thinking of the serve:

Step Two: Half-close your eyes and visualize your opponent as you just viewed him, letting him loom as an actual hazard. As you bounce the ball or change position, keep picturing your opponent's reaction.

Step Three: With that, picture your opponent, treating him as a dwindling factor much like the melting snowman. With your own actions, shift to the words *Relax—Relax* and the spelling R–E–L–A–X.

Step Four: As the opponent's figure fades and you visualize the empty court, open your eyes and focus on your target spot, ignoring your opponent entirely, as you switch the spelling from R–E–L–A–X to A–L–E–R–T.

Step Five: As you build the spelling of A–L–E–R–T into the word *Alert!*, take a deep breath and deliver your serve directly on target.

There is no set pattern to the steps just given, because they depend to a great degree upon the individual. A deliberate server would naturally take his time, while someone of a more energetic type would move into action faster. There is no harm in switching from one style to another, acting nervously or impatiently, even pausing and starting over. The main thing is to be yourself, but in doing so, shift the burden onto your opponent by disregarding him to such extent that your own ability seems all the greater in your own mind and therefore probably in his.

If you miss with your first serve, note how close to the line you came and gauge your second serve accordingly. Since this is a repeat of your previous try, you can almost duplicate the action, shading it just a trifle on the safe side while again dismissing your opponent as a dangerous factor.

When returning the serve, this technique can be used:

Step One: The receiver studies the server briefly, noting his preliminary stance, and adjusts his own position accordingly. Then, instead of thinking of the server as such:

Step Two: The receiver concentrates upon the probable course the server will follow, ignoring the server's actions to the point where he becomes a mechanical figure. The receiver then repeats "Relax—Relax," gradually slowing his pace into:

Step Three: This becomes the equivalent of the time-control technique used in trap-shooting, where your mind creates the impression that time itself is slackening with your count. As you scan the course the ball is to follow, you can picture its speed more as a lob than a drive as the server continues to gyrate in the background, until:

Step Four: As he tosses the ball and his arm goes up, you snap from relax into alert and follow the actual trajectory of the ball as it comes toward you. The larger the ball looms or the less its speed seems, the more effective your reaction will be. The same applies to your return stroke.

BALANCING YOUR PLAY BY INSTANT RECALL AND MENTAL PROJECTION

In both serving and receiving, competent tennis players are subject to a form of mental discipline that can be defined under the head of instant recall. This means that through constant practice they have developed their skill to the point where "motor memory" enables them to deliver an automatic muscular response. That is why the server can deliver a fast stroke just inside the line, while the receiver, if quick enough, can return the ball across the net in precisely the same fashion.

If such fast action continues, the players will need instant recall for each succeeding stroke; but the moment one player, through either luck or skill, places the ball almost beyond his opponent's reach, the situation shifts to mental projection. Assuming that you are the one who put your opponent in trouble, you no longer have to rely on instinct to handle his return stroke; you will have time to figure exactly where it will be coming and thereby rationalize your own return. For the first time in the rally—the exchange of strokes before a point is scored—you have a choice of what to do.

So you picture your next play in terms of your opponent's next reaction and keep on building it mentally, play by play, until you are so far ahead of him that all you need to do is deliver a smash shot at the proper juncture and the point is yours. That is, unless somewhere during the rally he manages to deliver a surprise stroke that forces you to rely on instant recall to counteract it. In that case, you must be sharp enough to begin the building process all over.

So much for tennis. Now let's apply the same principles to another sport.

□ BASEBALL: FROM LITTLE LEAGUE □
TO BIG LEAGUE

Like tennis, baseball begins with a confrontation between two opposing players, a pitcher and a batter. The basic purpose is similar in that the pitcher tries to throw the ball past the batter, who swings a bat in an effort to hit, but six or more pitches may be required. If the batter swings and misses, or refuses to swing at a good pitch, the result is called a strike, and with three strikes the batter is out. A bad pitch that the batter ignores is termed a ball, and after four of these the batter goes to first base. His main purpose is nevertheless to hit the ball into the playing field occupied by the opposing team and run to first base, where he is safe unless the ball is caught on the fly or thrown to the first baseman ahead of him. From there, he hopes to continue around the bases and score a run.

In baseball parlance, the thing a pitcher needs most is control in order to keep each pitch just within the strike zone, or close enough to get the batter to swing at a pitch that might otherwise be called a ball. Good pitching requires considerable skill and continued practice, which involve physical control as with balancing, juggling, or marksmanship. But the biggest factor is mental discipline, as any baseball fan will tell you. Often, a pitcher will go wild and walk two or three batters to first base; at other times he may settle down and strike out a formidable batter on three straight pitches.

I could cite many cases of big-league pitchers who have made a great start, then faded into oblivion; of others who have staged a comeback or accomplished wonders through a change of style; of still more who have jumped from obscurity to stardom; but most of all I have been impressed by those who just remained themselves, regardless of conditions. These are the pattern that all the rest should follow. I don't expect a lot of big-league pitchers to call me up to thank me for the advice, because few of them will follow it. But I do hope to receive letters over the years to come from little-league pitchers of today who have become the big-league pitchers of tomorrow, because by then they will realize that it was yesterday that they learned the technique of mental discipline.

My rule for such control is this: If you are in the pitcher's box, facing the first batter, take three deep breaths and ask yourself "Why am I here?"

Then wait for the true answer. It may be: *Because I'm the best pitcher on the team and they know it and I intend to prove it.*

If you are right, prove it. If you are wrong, do the *best you can* to pitch out of that hole. If they have to put in another pitcher, be thankful. Wish him well, because he is taking over the thing you couldn't do. There are eight other positions on the team, all open for somebody as good as you are, so take one of those.

With that attitude, you will be ready to combine the functions of mental discipline to the full. With teams that play only occasionally, you may be pitching because you talked yourself into it or because nobody else would take on the job, so you may have to visualize yourself as much better than you really are. But with any type of organized play, from little leagues on up through scholastic contests, you will be in there because the coach told you to pitch. Similarly, in semi-pro or big-league play, you may be the manager's choice for that particular game, so the burden is not all yours. Besides, you have a catcher who will call for the pitches he decides are best.

As a result of all those factors, you can concentrate on each pitch as though it represented the entire game. You can build such fantasy into reality by remembering that there have been instances when a new pitcher was called in to save a game and actually won it with a single pitch. So, having decided what your one pitch should be, you proceed: (1) To recall such pitches you have made before; then (2) to relax as you begin step: (3) then visualize your pitch following just the right trajectory with the batter swinging wildly; and (4) as you hear the echo of the imaginary baseball smacking into the catcher's mitt, you snap from relax to alert, and with it (5) you need only deliver the real pitch exactly as you pictured it.

These steps not only may vary with individual pitchers, they must also be adjusted according to the particular situation. Instead of ignoring the batter, include him in the scene, helping to activate it. The more he wags his real bat, hoping to disconcert you, the easier it is for you to imagine him taking a hopeless swing at a doozy curve or standing by dumfounded as your fast ball whizzes past him.

REVERSING THE PROCEDURE: BATTER VERSUS PITCHER

Only one player out of nine is a pitcher, but everybody on a team has to take his turn at bat, which means that there are many individual ways whereby a batter can worry a pitcher into putting the ball right where the batter wants it, or else pitching so many side ones that the batter gets a walk to first base. Originally, most batters choked the bat by holding it short so they could punch a pitch just out of a fielder's reach; but all that changed when the famous Babe Ruth set the pace for free swingers by knocking baseballs out of the ball park and thereby piling up records as a home-run hitter.

Babe Ruth originally was a pitcher, and unquestionably he used a mental-discipline formula to become one of the best in the game until his prowess as a hitter made him more valuable as an outfielder who took a regular turn at bat. When asked how he, as a free swinger, could match the high batting averages of most choke hitters, the Babe smilingly asserted that whenever he was in the batter's box, waiting for a pitch, "he could count every stitch on the baseball before it reached him." This was an exaggeration, naturally, but it fits perfectly with the slow-motion phase of our time control technique. Babe Ruth was a budding big-league player even in his boyhood; and with all the speed he could put behind his own pitches, he was never worried by another pitcher's fast ball when he was in the batter's box.

Proof was found in another of the Babe's sayings. When asked which of all the pitchers he ever faced had impressed him the most, he replied laconically: "They all looked alike to me." By combining those two elements, you have the Babe Ruth batting technique:

Upon taking your position in the batter's box: (1) Simply relax and swing your bat in whatever style suits you best, as (2) you watch the pitcher fidgeting about and reduce it to a mere mechanical action as you slow your relaxing count. (3) Timing your own action to the pitch, snap from relax into alert, (4) tighten your grip, and gauge your swing as the ball comes your way, either (5A) completing the swing to meet the ball with your bat or (5B) restraining your swing to let the pitch go by.

Batters who have used this technique have been amazed by how much steam a fast ball seemed to lose when they watched it closely instead of taking a hard swing blindly in hope of meeting it head-on. Others have been even more astounded when they saw what they *thought* was a pitcher's fast ball come floating up to the plate. In their efforts to step up their reactions, they were adding speed to the pitches themselves. In contrast, some players, instead of trying to become sluggers, have developed a "camera eye" that enables them to tell good pitches from bad and thus wait out a pitcher until he gives them just what they want. All these techniques apply to fielders as well as batters. Recall, projection, and timing make the game of baseball an ideal type of mind conditioner. As tension mounts among the spectators, it should lessen with the players, who follow the Relax–Alert formula to the even dropping the x as they spring to action: R–E–L–A–L–E–R–T, faster than you can spell it.

The same principles can be applied to other popular sports. The most striking example is basketball.

□ BASKETBALL □

In this game, two points are scored for a toss through the basket in the course of active play, with a single point for a shot made from the foul line during a brief time out. Back when scoring was low in basketball, much of the shooting was hit-or-miss and tension would mount when a nervous player went to the foul line to make a crucial free throw. As the speed of the modern game increased and scores rose to ever–higher figures, accuracy developed proportionately. That made mental discipline a dominant factor in which the foul throw can serve as the basis.

Picture yourself at the foul line, practicing free throws. Each becomes more and more a replica of the others that preceded it, until the foul-line toss is almost second nature. To avoid tension, you can begin with the Relax–Alert procedure, but as your efficiency increases you can apply full-fledged mental imagery, utilizing the twin functions of recall and projection.

As you face the basket, instead of gauging the shot, tossing it, and watching for the result, half-close your eyes and (1) take three deep breaths as you (2) think back to perfect practice shots you have already made; then (3) as you feel your hands coming up in response, switch from recall to projection by imagining that the ball is leaving your hands and (4) following the exact arc needed to carry it through the basket so perfectly that (5) your final image shows the net barely wavering as the ball drops through for the goal.

Repeat this a few times and as you come to the third or middle step, you will find that as the lifting impression increases, it will merge with the rise of the ball. That becomes your *moment of precision.* Recall from the past becomes the projection of the future. Open your eyes fully, focus on the basket, take another deep breath, and make the actual toss exactly as you imagined it.

Continue this until your physical practice and mental imagery blend completely and you will find that instead of hesitating or pushing ahead, your big moment will be the deciding factor that will put precision in your toss. Once you have reached that stage, you can gradually reduce the preliminaries and apply the system with exactitude during an actual game.

APPLYING THE MOMENT OF PRECISION TO ACTIVE PLAY

Familiarity with foul shooting can reach the point where you might walk up to the foul line and toss a basket as you arrived there. However, by speeding the process, you might also ruin it, so there would be no sense in missing a foul shot by being too sure of yourself or trying to show off. But in regular play you are often forced to speed your action, and when that occurs you will find that you can still apply the system to scoring goals from the court.

To do so, you must speed your mental imagery as well as your physical action. Your process becomes: instant recall—moment of precision—spontaneous projection, sometimes in such close-knit style that all three seem simultaneous. That can happen when you make a shot from under the basket, a spot that is often as familiar as the foul line. With not an instant to lose, you repeat a toss you have often used before, letting automatic precision produce the anticipated result.

You will have more time, however, with a set shot that you make from a familiar position during a free moment. Here the analogy to the foul line is perfect; in some cases, in fact, it is practically the same thing, provided you remember that you must get the shot away or else you can forget it. I have known skilled basketball players whose keen-triggered minds can run the gamut of recall—precision—projection in split seconds while they are putting those impressions into action.

Recall alone can often trigger the action. A keen player, finding a sudden opportunity that he had before, goes into a moment of precision without projecting his mind toward the result. Conversely, in the course of play, that same player can look ahead to a chance to place himself in a spot where he can receive a pass and turn it into an immediate shot for an almost certain goal. There, recall plays virtually no part before precision takes over, but the credit still belongs to projection.

I have cited these in detail, because the elements of recall, precision, and projection, particularly when combined in instant, momentary, and spontaneous form, play a major role in other fast-moving sports besides basketball. Their cultivation through such sports can enable the individual to gain great presence of mind that will be invaluable on and off the courts.

□ 14 □

UTILIZING MENTAL DISCIPLINE IN STUDIES

The question I am asked most often during my college tours is "How can I do better in my studies?" It is put by students at every level, from college freshmen to those taking graduate courses. Often, those making high marks are the ones most anxious to know. That is not surprising. Some students feel (and perhaps correctly!) that they are lucky to have gotten by as well as they have, which makes their apprehension all the more understandable.

As their extracurricular activities increase, many students find it harder to keep up with their work. This makes them look for shortcuts, particularly at examination time. They "cram" in an emergency; and once they begin to apply that practice to several subjects at once, they find themselves in trouble.

I always feel sorry for the student who did so well in high school he didn't need to study very much, and later becomes a problem student at the college level because he has never developed proper study habits. Others with high IQs have a capacity for learning that does not go beyond the range of high-school subjects. In short, although a college education should be available to all, it is not the answer for everyone.

The idea that everyone must go to college to succeed is greatly overstressed. Many people have manual skills or natural talents and can make it on their own without the label of a degree. To name all the other dormant assets people have would be superfluous because they are things that people discover themselves. But the sure way to meet challenging studies and increase confidence is through the development of mental discipline.

Start with the basic key of concentration and practice the exercises given there. Apply the power of concentration through visual imagery and continue on through mind expansion. By putting the inner mind to work, you will reach the true stage of contemplation that every student should attain. Memory training may also prove to be an important study aid.

Once you have practiced various mind-conditioning techniques regularly over a period of a few weeks or longer, you should have access to an inner level of thinking that should enable you to concentrate on your studies to an appreciable and gratifying degree. Your next step is to apply yourself to your studies even more strongly. To do that, I have frequently recommended a special five-minute conditioning exercise which should be repeated two to three times a day:

Assume a comfortable seated position in a chair so that you can (1) lean back and rest your hands *palms upward* in your lap, keeping them far enough apart so they are not touching. (2) To be well aware of their position, you can slide your hands slightly forward toward your knees; then (3) as you relax, without looking at your hands, half-close your eyes and draw a deep breath. (4) Hold it momentarily, then exhale easily and gradually. (5) Repeat this simple breathing exercise and (6) by the end of the fifth breath you will find that your hands tend to turn inward automatically and fall into your lap.

This spontaneous reaction indicates that you have coordinated mental and physical relaxation to a degree that represents a mood for study. Don't try to force it; if you don't succeed, keep repeating it until you do, or give it up for the time being. Moving your hands farther forward or closer together may help, provided they do not touch at the outset, though that does not matter after they turn inward and downward, since they may then come together automatically. You will then know that although you are relaxed, you can key yourself to mental effort without becoming tense. Otherwise, the attempt to study could defeat itself, since a certain amount of tension is unconsciously involved. If you feel that you are losing your mood for study, you can revert to the conditioning process just described, although after a time you may find it unnecessary.

Having fitted yourself into a middle norm free from emotional extremes and therefore conducive to study, you should contemplate your purpose: to learn what you are studying. You must (1) absorb the material successfully and (2) retain it sufficiently, so that (3) later on, in a test situation, you will be able to recall it. If you have applied the elements of this procedure to mental-discipline techniques given in the earlier chapters, you will grasp the study situation to perfection. Every student must literally "box in" what he intends to learn, so that no essential details can later escape him. Concentration, imagery, expansion, memory, contemplation, and all other functions of the inner mind become the ever-handy tools that help fulfill the task.

The preliminary step is to gather all the necessary study material and arrange it in proper and convenient order. I call this preliminary because it is largely a routine function, but it is highly essential to good results, because without it, a student can fall prey to procrastination, overrationalization, and trivial distractions.

Let's assume you have gained a sufficient degree of self-confidence to proceed with a programmed mode of study. If necessary, you can refresh yourself with the two-week formula for self-confidence (pages 153–154) by reciting "Kreskin's conditioning is becoming deeply entrenched in my unconscious."

APPLYING CONCENTRATION TO SET THE MIND'S COURSE

Now you are ready to apply full concentration to your studies. You do not have to concern yourself with how well you can concentrate. You have already gained the required ability through exercises in mental discipline, ranging from the basic procedures in Chapter 1 to the Kreskin formula for self-confidence, which can be applied as an update "refresher." You now proceed to establish what I term a "mind set" to activate your powers of concentration. This is done through the following technique:

Step One: While sitting, take a pad and pencil and write a positive, constructive suggestion that says in essence: *The material I am about to study is going to make a deep and lasting impression on my mind, so absorbed will I be in it.*

Step Two: Read this back so you can remember it, which is why your own wording is best, because it will spring more easily to mind. In reading it, concentrate on the fact that *those very words* represent the first of the "deep and lasting impressions" to be imbedded in your mind, thereby setting your mind for all that are to follow.

Step Three: After reading the message, lay it in your lap and assume a comfortable position, letting your hands rest palms upward, so you can refer to your paper if you need to while you repeat your statement to yourself three times, moving your lips but not speaking out loud.

Step Four: Now center your attention on a spot just in front of you, which may be some item in the study material. Go into the Relax–Alert procedure by taking five deep breaths and holding the fifth as you mentally spell R–E–L–A–X.

Step Five: Exhale as you relax and let your hands fall inward—which they should do of their own accord—and resume your breathing normally while remaining perfectly, passively relaxed, letting random words of the written suggestion reverberate around and around in your mind without concentrating on it. Keep your eyes closed as further impressions come to mind.

At this point there is a time lapse (the length of which will depend on the individual student) that is an important feature. You may note that the procedure so far represents a blend of various exercises described earlier, all focused on the same objective—relaxation as an aid to study. The difference will depend partly on one's familiarity with the various exercises and partly on individual reactions. For some, the written suggestion will predominate, so they should wait until it dwindles. For others, jumbled impressions may take over, so they should wait until those clear. Still others may feel a pressing urge to get on with their studies; ordinarily this is a good sign unless the student was definitely worried to begin with. (In that case, he or she should start the process all over.)

Some have actually trained themselves to handle this situation, and all who utilize this study exercise regularly will sooner or later approach that stage. In any case, you end your period of relaxation when you simply feel that your time is up. Remember you've trained yourself to unconsciously judge the time it would ordinarily take to count slowly from 50 to 0; like the soft melt of wax.

Step Six: Spell the letters in reverse, counting them as you would numbers, slowly, emphatically: A–L–E–R–T, and with your final breath, pronounce the word *Alert!* NOTE: Some persons have visualized Steps 5 and 6 as one, with the words spelled clear across: R–E–L–A–X–A–L–E–R and the mind wiping them out letter by letter, then adding a final T and pronouncing the word *Alert!*

Step Seven: Open your eyes and proceed with your planned study, laying your written message on the desk with your work to serve as a later remainder.

When you conclude your first study period and go over the material, you proceed to lock it in your mind by a postsuggestion process that resembles your original exercise in brief, but with certain important differences:

Step One: Take a fresh sheet of paper and write a new message, also positive in wording, to this effect: *The material I have just studied has made such a deep and lasting impression on my mind that I can use it, recall it, and handle it any time I wish.*

Steps Two, Three, and Four are repetitions of the original procedure, but involve the new statement instead of the old. They lead directly into:

Step Five, which in this instance is brief and represents the final step. As you exhale and relax, letting your hands fall inward, you can open your eyes soon after the words of the new message reverberate in your mind, as your one purpose is to plant it there.

Quite a few students abbreviate this postsuggestion exercise by simply repeating the new statement aloud instead of writing it, but it is usually preferable to use the written suggestion, particularly during your first trials. You will then have both sheets available after you have taken your break and prepare for your next study period. Thus your procedure will be letter-perfect on each occasion. During your break, you can do whatever you want for fifteen minutes or longer: watch television, have a sandwich, call up a friend, or the like, provided you do not become too deeply involved in anything that will upset your planned schedule.

After your break you should be ready to come back and attack each segment of your studies, giving yourself the before-study suggestion, going through the deep-breathing exercises clear to the word *Alert!* that marks the start of Step 6, which launches you into actual study. You close that off when you finish your poststudy suggestion, concluding the entire study session.

UTILIZING RECOGNITION AND REPETITION IN REVIEW

In the study process just described, the emphasis on the two written statements sums up the situation perfectly. With one, you *set your mind* to a definite purpose at the conscious level; with the other, you *locked in* the material thus learned, storing it in your unconscious. Now comes the all-important sequel of reactivating it through recall, according to your own stated objective.

Under certain conditions this can be almost automatic. Years ago, a craftsman often followed a single trade and a scholar devoted his career to a specialized subject. In the whirl of modern life, varieties of interest render this impossible. Subjects taught in schools and colleges are so varied that they often crowd one another out of a student's mind. That can be counteracted through a regulated process of review, which not only serves as a refresher but can often provide an added stimulus toward total recall as well.

If you study during the day, you can review a subject late in the evening, while a subject studied in the evening can be reviewed the next morning. If you are studying a subject a few days ahead, you have more leeway, but don't let a highly

important subject go too long, because you may want to review it a second time. In all cases, your procedure should
follow this pattern:

Step One: Assume a comfortable position, eyes half-closed,
and picture yourself studying as you did in actuality. Take it
slowly, maintaining a state of *relaxation,* which merges into:

Step Two: Go over the actual data you studied, either briefly
or in detail, but adhering closely to your actual process of
study, visualizing as you mentally list the highlights through
repetition.

Step Three: Let the details grow and expand themselves to
the point questions and answers come to mind spontaneously
and you find yourself reciting facts you have learned, approaching a state of full *recall.*

Step Four: Take a few deep breaths, open your eyes, and
make notes of the results either mentally or with pad and
pencil, thus completing your *review.*

Don't expect this to be letter-perfect on the first try. You
may not have set your mind strongly enough at the start, thus
failing to acquire all the data you should have; or you may
have locked in facts so hurriedly that you forgot the combination. Either way, an intelligent, unbiased appraisal will
show you where you fell short.

Perhaps your studies demand more concentration on your
part. Possibly you should devote more time to visual imagery
or inner-mind development. Maybe you should delve deeper
into contemplation. Or it could be that memory methods
would be your best answer. Anything from catch phrases to a
pictorial key list may help bridge the gap between study and

review, as represented by relaxation and recall, with repetition in between.

In any event, after every *study exercise,* allow a sufficient time lapse for a *review exercise.* Continue that procedure throughout the college term, improving your technique as you proceed by simply following the recommended methods—with which, by now, you should be thoroughly acquainted. They will condition you for the climax:

HOW TO PASS EXAMS WITH GREATER PRECISION AND EASE

When examinations loom, the principles of mental discipline seemingly become far more important than during the course of ordinary study, although the two are actually closely interwoven. That fact, however, is so generally overlooked that even some of the best of students ask my advice on how to counteract the strain and stress that confront them at examination time.

Their problem is simply this: All during the semester they have been getting by without applying themselves fully. Even if they have been utilizing mental discipline, they may have neglected certain phases, particularly where review exercises are involved. They have done well in the classroom, but in daily sessions only; if they had been called upon to go over the same ground a few weeks later, they would have found that many essential facts had slipped from their minds.

When exams approach, these students take for granted that they know more than they actually do. That in turn causes them to regard the coming exam merely as a collection of trifling assignments rolled into one big one, which can be handled both rapidly and smoothly. Therefore they allot what they regard as sufficient time for final study and often postpone that study on the assumption that the closer it comes to exam time the better, since all the vital facts will then be fresh in mind. But when they get down to work, instead of smooth running they encounter snags that slow their pace and turn their normal form of study into a grind. With time running out, they are confronted by a cram situation. This frantic, last-minute rush leaves them unequipped for the examination.

There are two simple ways to counteract this. One is to give constant attention to mental-discipline techniques during the course of regular study, with special emphasis on review exercises. Before starting a new study session it is always a very good plan to review the previous assignment, if only briefly. This tells you how well your power of recall is functioning; it forms a lasting link between the old and new; and it serves as a warm-up for the work to come, thus saving time in actual study while producing more results. The other important factor is to allow more than ample time in studying for the examination itself and to treat that study as a special type by interlocking or interchanging the factors of study and review, so that they become a composite exercise:

Step One: Gather your material and assume a comfortable position as if to begin a regular study period, saying mentally: *I am now about to recall material that has made such a lasting impression on my mind that I can revive it and review it at will.*

Step Two: Utilize the Relax-Alert procedure by taking five deep breaths, spelling R–E–L–A–X and letting your hands fail inward, but in this case go immediately into:

Step Three: As you take a deep breath, spell A–L–E–R–T, adding the word *Alert!* Having used this process regularly, you are on familiar ground and can merge promptly into a mood of full recall, as described in the reviewing exercise (page 190).

Step Four: Now, studying the material before you, keep two words in mind: *revive* and *review*. Do not stress them; think of them like left and right or up and down or in and out, so you can apply your mind consciously to the material while sorting it unconsciously into two special categories.

Thus, in your own customary form of study, you are listing under REVIVE the facts that start to come to mind and under REVIEW those that are already there. Whether you do this mentally or mark an actual checklist, the result is the same. Automatically you program yourself for the immediate task ahead: to *strengthen* whatever you are *reviving,* while *reviewing* whatever you have *strengthened.* That way, you avoid unnecessary effort as well as unnecessary anguish.

Run through that process speedily and smoothly. No snags, no slowdowns. Then go back and pick up the REVIVE data, like a new study, and you will find that you can split them into REVIVE and REVIEW. Do this a few times and you will have it made. Don't worry about snags or roadblocks. By avoiding them to start, you can go back and pick up where you left off, finding them all the easier just because you have. The upshot: You turn REVIVE into REVIEW. That puts you in.

To prepare for the exam, find a place where you can be alone, whether in your room in the dorm, in an empty classroom, or lounging on the lawn. Go through the contemplation exercise—take five deep breaths, and relax with your eyes closed. Do not employ the backward count, but fill your mind's void with pieces of the suggestion as they come into your mind. At the end of the time, count from one to five and open your eyes; or if you have become accustomed to spelling A–L–E–R–T, you may do so.

Repeat: *The material I have revived and reviewed will come to me during my examination quickly and easily. It will spring up whenever I need it, because it has been there all along.*

It will work. I know, not only because I have tried it, but also because those to whom I have described it have tried it too, with the same positive results. Sometimes, from their reports, they have gotten those results faster than I did—which makes me all the happier.

□ 15 □

MAKING AND BREAKING HABITS

Anyone who has utilized the exercises leading from concentration into contemplation through visual imagery, dilemma-solving, and decision-making will have acquired worthwhile abilities that can serve as safeguards against undesirable behavior patterns. But you can fortify yourself even further by extending your inner-mind power into new and productive areas.

HOW TO DEVELOP AND UTILIZE AN ALARM-CLOCK MIND
Proof of the power of the inner mind is found in the fact that certain persons have the seemingly uncanny ability to awaken themselves at whatever hour in the morning they have decided upon the night before. Even stranger than the ability itself is the fact that it is latent in many individuals who have never realized that their minds, too, can function in such a manner. Of the various approaches to develop this ability, the most satisfactory is the deep contemplation–relaxation technique:

Step One: Before retiring, take a slip of paper and write down the time you want to awaken in the morning—say, seven o'clock. Keep this in mind until your actual bedtime; then proceed with:

Step Two: Say to yourself, slowly and emphatically: "I shall awaken in the morning, becoming wide awake, at seven o'clock." Repeat this twice, making three times in all; then make yourself comfortable.

Step Three: Take five deep breaths, closing your eyes as you do. At the end of the fifth, spell R–E–L–A–X like a slow countdown, repeating the spelling while exhaling normally and finally concluding with the word *Relax*.

Step Four: Keeping your eyes closed, allow the time "seven o'clock" to reverberate in your mind while you are getting into bed. When the image of time no longer enters your thoughts, just forget about it and doze.

Many people have been amazed by the regularity with which this system works; some have added variations to intensify the process, one effective way being to draw a clock dial with the hands at seven o'clock instead of writing the words, or in addition to the words. Another method is to set an actual alarm clock at the desired time instead of writing the time or drawing the diagram. I have met people who have said that they frequently awakened just before the alarm went off by using that method. I have personally programmed myself to the point that before I turn the light out, I simply close my eyes and picture the hands of a clock at the time I wish to waken; I then turn out the light, think of it once more, and then forget about it, only to find myself waking at that time!

Theorists have come up with many reasons why people are able to do this. One psychologist has claimed that the mind has an inborn timing mechanism that enables the individual to gauge time unconsciously. Actually, there has not been sufficient evidence that such could be the case without some outside help toward which the mind could give attention. The ticking of an actual clock, for example, would serve as evidence that time was passing, but it would take more than that for the mind to estimate the exact hour, unless the individual's level of sleep lightens around the time he wants to waken and he may inadvertently half-open his eyes so that he can see the clock.

Another theory is that the individual has become used to certain sounds or activities about him at different times of the morning. In the past, many people unconsciously realized that the milkman would be delivering bottles around six-thirty in the morning and the resulting clatter furnished the cue that the waking time was only a half-hour off, which was easy to judge during a light level of sleep. Today, it is highly probable that we are using stimuli around us that we don't think about in waking life—that birds may start chirping at a certain time of the year; that the sun comes up earlier in the spring and later in the fall; that household activities in a home, or the increasing rumbles of elevators in an apartment building can tell their tale in a very graphic way.

This brings up two extremes. First, the person living in a quiet community where a distant bell chimes the hours. He wakes up at half-past seven every morning because he has been half-awake all night, counting off the hours without realizing it. When the clock chimes seven, he starts counting minutes instead of hours, so he is naturally wide awake at seven-thirty. The other extreme is the hermit living in a cave where no light or sound can possibly enter to disturb his life as a total recluse. Such a person obviously has a tremendous misconception of time—as we know it. I have added that last phrase because, for all we know, he might be the one person who would wake up totally triggered for the day to come.

Between the extremes there are further phases of the alarm-clock theme, marking it as a still more important adjunct of mind development. Even if you do depend on an alarm clock or a member of your family to wake you up at home, or leave a call at a motel desk when traveling, you still should condition your mind in the manner I have prescribed for two reasons: (1) because it is a good way to develop the technique, since it relieves your mind from any worry about actually awakening; (2) since your mind is set for a certain hour, your sleep tends to gauge itself accordingly, which means that you probably will be fully refreshed when you awaken, which in itself is sufficient reason to make a steady practice of this technique.

There is still more to be gained, because the technique can be applied on a short range as well as an overnight basis. If you feel like a nap in the afternoon, you can take it knowing that you will not oversleep; if you are tired while working in the evening, yet still want to go on, you take a few hours sleep and pick things up from there. This was the method used by Thomas Edison, who in his later years literally worked around the clock, alternating his hours of wakefulness and sleep to gain the best from both, a process to which he attributed some of his greatest inventions.

In addition, the alarm-clock principle can be used to cultivate a time sense during waking hours. You can set an hour for an appointment and go about your daily routine knowing that you will sense the right time as it approaches. You can regulate your coffee break and your lunch hour precisely. No longer will there be the mad rush to get to parties in the evening or the deep regret that you didn't leave sooner after the party was really over. By acquiring the alarm-clock habit and checking it to avoid errors as you go along, you can increase your efficiency to a high degree and your mental attitude to a point far beyond.

☐ CULTIVATING GOOD HABITS TO ☐
WEED OUT BAD HABITS

I have delved deeply into the cultivation of a time sense because it represents a prime example of how the conscious focusing of attention on a good habit can enable your unconscious to take over and render the process automatic.

This is like the growing of plants or flowers, which presents problems when you find that weeds are growing among them. There is only one thing to do with weeds; get rid of them—and the same applies to habits. To cultivate the good, weed out the bad. The best example is that of smoking, since tobacco itself is commonly classed as a weed. In the case of cigarette smoking, which is the most widespread phase of the tobacco habit and generally conceded to be the most injurious, the contemplation–relaxation approach is the best, although certain tools can also be used during the day to remind one that his or her purpose is to cut down the habit.

The most realistic procedure in the majority of cases is the gradual overcoming of the cigarette habit, a technique I utilized for years when I worked with a clinical psychologist. The first condition is that the individual must truly want to stop smoking. If he has a half-hearted feeling about this, it just can't happen, because he must learn to respond to his own ideas and a half-hearted response is not sufficient. Once he has expressed a real desire to stop, it can be further encouraged as he proceeds and he is ready for the gradual-overcoming approach as a starter.

Assume that an individual habitually smokes a pack of twenty cigarettes a day. Each night, he is to place a full pack of cigarettes by his bedside. Now, before going to sleep, he uses the deep contemplation–relaxation approach, utilizing the following steps: (1) Focusing his mind upon the pack of cigarettes, he begins a slow countdown: 20–19–18–17–16–15

—and stops right there. He repeats this, visualizing cigarettes instead of numbers, as often as he wants, always ending on fifteen. Then (2) he repeats to himself, over and over, "I am going to find fifteen cigarettes more than enough for me." As he tires of this, he can stress *more than enough,* thus subtly gaining a vague distaste for some of the cigarettes. Finally (3) he takes his five deep breaths, spells out R–E–L–A–X— *Relax!* and prepares for sleep.

In the morning, he naturally recalls his decision of the night before. Since the pack is on the table to confirm it, he opens the pack and counts out five cigarettes, laying them aside for the day. That leaves him with a pack of only fifteen, and he is fully aware that those *fifteen cigarettes* are to last him through the day. To drive that home, he should repeat the contemplation–relaxation exercise of the night before, again stressing that one particular phrase and adding still another: "I am going to find fifteen cigarettes *more than enough* for me—although there may be a mild distaste about them."

He goes through his daily activities, recognizing that he has to limit himself to fifteen cigarettes. This is a technique in itself, the most important part being to become more conscious every time he is about to smoke or decides to smoke. This means that he is learning to *become attentive* to his habit. There is something very peculiar and at the same time highly enlightening about being attentive to a habit, because a habit is basically unconscious activity such as muscular movement or mental detachment. By becoming aware of what he is doing, he is actually shaking off the habit to a certain degree because he is no longer unaware of it. In most cases of smoking (though this will not work with all), the individual will find himself working to enjoy smoking these fifteen cigarettes since he must be careful not to waste them.

Becoming conscious of every aspect of the cigarette, most notably its fragrance, he finds it easy to note a distasteful quality. He will also become aware of what he is doing before he reaches for the pack, which hand he is using, which pocket it is in and why. In so doing he is unconsciously releasing the hold the habit has on him. When he is going for a cigarette, he will reflect whether he really needs it, since he only has fifteen, although they should be more than enough for him. Like many people, in reaching for the pack out of habit, he wouldn't have appreciated the smoking of the entire allowance until now, when his quota is limited.

If he does this for one week, restricting himself to fifteen cigarettes a day, the next week he can decrease the number to ten, then in another week to five, and then he should try to cut it out entirely. He can do so if a distaste for those "few extra" cigarettes continues, because by the final week the distasteful cigarettes will be the only ones he has in his depleted pack of five. But it doesn't always work that easily: for some smokers, the law of scarcity may cause them to value the last few cigarettes all the more.

The awareness technique can still take care of that, because it finds ways to undermine the habit. The important thing is to keep applying all the desirable approaches: practicing the contemplation–relaxation exercise each night, feeding in the autosuggestion of more than enough, then the morning practice with the autosuggestion again. As a follow-up, by starting out with a new pack every night, the subject will find that at the end of three days, he will have fifteen left-over cigarettes, enough for him to rebuild a pack of fifteen and save what would have been the cost of an entire pack back in the old twenty-a-day period.

If he starts out as a two-pack smoker, he will cut to thirty-five cigarettes during the first week, unless he decides to take five from each pack and go with thirty. Otherwise, the procedure is much the same, but there is one factor that may occur in both cases. When a smoker cuts from twenty to fifteen, he is eliminating a *quarter* of his daily supply; from fifteen to ten, a *third;* and from ten to five, a *half*. This will make him value his remaining cigarettes more, and by the time he is down to five, he may regard that as an irreducible minimum. To break the habit entirely, other incentives must be added, such as:

Higher purpose, or the benefits gained by the nonsmoker. His food will taste better; he will gain the benefit of fresh air. He can picture himself as an athlete in training, out to make the team. If he is a heavy smoker, the matter of economy can enter—saving money is a lot better than saving cigarette coupons. The problem here is getting past the first few weeks, because the smoker who tries to quit cold often gives up. That can be helped by:

Mental projection, where the smoker keeps picturing how he will feel three weeks from now when he can look back and realize that he has really kicked the habit. Each day he foregoes smoking entirely he is that much closer to his goal. Training, camping, and working on jobs where smoking is not allowed can all help such an effort.

Increased aversion: This can prove a great booster to the awareness technique. Once a smoker feels that his pack contains more than enough cigarettes for the day, he can turn his mild distaste into actual dislike and finally disgust. This is used in so-called demonstrations of "hypnotism" where people are convinced that cigarettes are utterly distasteful and therefore let their imagination do the rest. In some cases, they are given a cigarette containing a horsehair, which really does taste terrible when they try to smoke it. Such demonstrations soon wear off, however, and become less effective when repeated, since it is like going over old ground. But if the smoker can pick up the suggestion and keep applying it to himself, his continued aversion may very well carry him over the trial period needed to break the habit completely.

Fear of consequences dates back to the very early days of cigarette smoking when cigarettes were nicknamed "coffin nails" because each was a token of a shortening life span. This method of discouraging smoking was long ago abandoned as both futile and ridiculous, but it is gaining real impact as a result of scientific findings and official warnings against the injurious results of excessive smoking. If a long-term smoker interprets "excessive" as being retroactive, he may feel that he has gone beyond his allotted total and therefore be ready to quit tomorrow.

□ APPLYING HABIT-BREAKING RULES □

In a habit such as nail-biting, the awareness technique will tend to undermine the automatic nature of the habit as effectively as with smoking. Similar conditioning using the contemplation–relaxation technique can be applied in such cases. Just as a smoker who reaches for a cigarette pack decides to put it away for the time being, a nail-biter can relax and be satisfied by merely drawing a fingernail lightly between his teeth. Other habits may be similarly reduced.

Some habits, however, can have deep-seated causes, which means that there should be consultations with psychotherapists to understand the causes; otherwise the use of the usual habit-breaking techniques may prove ineffective. Yet even stammering, which so often has a strongly psychological cause, can be helped and even overcome through mind-conditioning exercises that reduce tension. One proof of this is that you can actually quick-talk the average person into stammering by confusing him with a barrage of words and demanding prompt answers. It is therefore logical that, if tension contributes to stammering, by turning it the other way about and putting the habitual stammerer totally at ease, stammering would be reduced. There is a good test here: When people who stammer talk to friends in a darkened room, their stammering may cease. When that occurs, you know it is a nervous habit that can be overcome; if it doesn't, it belongs in the psychotherapeutic or even physical therapy departments.

□   HOW TO LOSE WEIGHT   □

If you wish to diet successfully, you must realize it is your mind that supplies the motivation necessary to achieve weight loss. Only if you have a deep motivation can you make dieting work.

Motivations are poorly understood even today, but we do know that some people are only bothered by excess weight on a surface level; for these people the job of conjuring up strong motivations will be difficult. Also, there are those whose excess weight actually fulfills some unconscious need. Therefore serious weight problems should be referred to a competent doctor.

For the average person, however, here are some of my favorite techniques for achieving weight loss.

THE MIRROR IMAGE

Among the methods of thinking yourself thin through constant autosuggestion is the mirror image. It was devised almost accidentally by a salesman in a deluxe men's shop who used to watch customers admire themselves in new suits while standing in front of a three-way mirror. The salesman was putting on weight and when he looked at himself in the mirror his self-admiration became self-criticism. Each day he would look at himself and think how much better he would look if he lost weight. He would attribute the excess weight to things he had eaten or to lack of exercise. Soon he was putting himself in a mood to diet and getting results. Even better, he described his mirror method to his portly customers and showed them clothes that they could get if they weighed less, and this began to work; it even brought him more business.

You can do the same thing through mental imagery. Picture yourself in front of a three-way mirror and imagine yourself thinner than you are. Double-check your weight on the scales every few days. Then do the image exercise, visualizing yourself wearing a new suit a size smaller.

The leave-out method. You simply set a normal amount that you would like to eat but realize that you have to cut down. So breakfast, for example, is fruit, cereal, eggs, and toast. Lunch is appetizer, entrée, dessert. Dinner is soup, entrée, salad, and dessert. Now you cut out one item on each, say cereal, dessert, soup. Keep the food. Put it in the refrigerator. Have it handy, telling yourself you will eat it later if you get hungry midmorning, midafternoon, or evening. If you are busy you will probably forget it, or someone else may eat it. Pretty soon you are cutting down almost automatically because you are dropping these side dishes along the way.

Hunger vs. appetite. Decide to eat *only* when hunger demands. When you want to eat or think of something edible or smell something cooking, ask yourself, do you really need it?

Keeping a diet diary. This is an excellent aid to losing weight. List what you ate, whether you ate too much, how much you enjoyed it, why you took extra bread (maybe because the soup hadn't been served or whatever).

Brag about what you passed up. Go through a contemplation exercise. Think over meals you cut down on. Picture an evening meal and how you can get out of eating too much.

All of us have had the experience of regretting a big meal we ate, but there are also cases of people who have dreamed about eating a big meal after going to sleep hungry and woke up feeling quite satisfied.

Picture a feast instead of raiding the refrigerator. If it carries on into your dreams, so much the better.

Place a picture of yourself on your refrigerator. Try to diet with other people. Get your friends to lose weight with you. In dieting we need constant reminders.

If you are on a diet or wish to diet, take a mental trip in which you pretend to be turned off by a particular food that you can't resist; imagine that the food is infected with worms, and as you eat it the repulsive little worms crawl out of your mouth and all over your body, or pretend that you are drowning in your favorite food. Sometimes, too much of a good thing is almost repulsive; so if you imagine the favorite food as overwhelming you or just too much, or grossly rampant about you, you may begin to become turned off by that food, for you can try to enjoy something too much in the area of eating. If you are on a diet you should always, in using your imagination on a mental trip, seek to picture yourself as looking the way you are planning to look and imagining your friends honoring you or complimenting you on your new look, what you are wearing; that is, your future aim. You should learn to relax completely by attending to different parts of your body; first of all, tensing them and then relaxing them, including facial muscles, neck muscles, shoulders, arms, forearms, hands, the frowning of the face, the tightening of the jaw, the wrinkling of the nose, the whole thing of it, for a few seconds, and suddenly relaxing. This, done through the body, the arching of the back, the raising of the chest, pushing shoulders back as hard as you can for a few seconds, and relaxing, next, the stomach, the abdomen, feet, legs, inevitably tensing the entire body after doing each part of relaxing and then, all at once, tensing the entire body and relaxing completely. This three or four minutes of physical exercise followed by mental exercise and a projection of your future appearance, of how you will look and feel, and reflecting upon why should help you to handle diets with success.

□ 16 □

PERSONALITY DEVELOPMENT THROUGH MENTAL DISCIPLINE

We come now to the ultimate in mental discipline, the development of an outer personality through the functions of the inner mind. In a certain sense, this can be classed as a form of visual imagery with you as a target or focal point, but it cannot stop there. You must see yourself as a dilemma-solver and a decision-maker as well; in fact, you must review and reenact every phase of mind conditioning from concentration through to contemplation, utilizing the methods you have gained along the way. But the application of these techniques is not the present issue. Your concern now is to avoid the pitfalls that might render your actions inadequate or ineffective by detracting from the outer personality you are trying to create.

That is what I mean by the balance that everyone should not only try to attain, but can attain, by simply keeping at it. Unfortunately, most people usually fall short of the mark because they think they have attained it before they really have. They are not really to blame, however, because they have not been subjected to a sufficiently rigid test. To illustrate this, I shall cite the case of two lawyers—Andrew and Zachary—with whose careers I have been closely familiar and to whom I have given those names because they were actually as far apart as the letters A and Z.

Andrew was a gentleman of the old school who felt that he could best state his case by being himself. When he stepped before a judge and jury, he became himself at what he pictured was his absolute best but really was his worst. Feeling that he had impressed everyone by his inner sincerity, he began to hem and haw, finally coming to the point he wanted to put across, then indulging in some trifling but friendly comments that missed the point entirely. He kept on with this routine until the court was totally bored; then he wrapped it up with a sudden flare that made the listeners feel he was the man they wanted to go along with, provided nobody else put up a better argument. Usually, nobody else did.

Zachary had modern ideas. He wanted to be the man the judge and—particularly—the jury thought he was. He wound himself up like a clock and let go, thinking that they would regard him as the self he wanted them to think he was, which they did, until the clockwork ran down. Even then he wasn't beaten; for the first time, he became himself and apologized for the mechanical failure and won everyone to his way of thinking through a frank display of his inner sincerity.

People who knew both Andrew and Zachary always wished that they would meet in actual conflict, on the chance that each would have then appreciated the other's viewpoint and could have borrowed enough from it to have improved his own status. But they were operating in too limited an area: in the case of a courtroom, arena might have been a better term. No matter what the outcome, whoever won or lost, Zachary would still have referred to Andrew as a doddering old idiot and Andrew would have called Zachary a bombastic windbag.

How can you avoid this pitfall if it happens to be in your path to success? By following two simple rules: Try to see yourself as others see you; then try to see others as others see them. A lawyer can do well to picture himself first as a judge, then as a juror, watching himself in action from their viewpoints. Then he should continue to play the parts of judge and juror while considering an opposing attorney's arguments. I have given this advice to lawyers who were really counterparts of Andrew and Zachary but were still young enough to recognize its worth.

The same applies to people in all walks of public life, and in business and private life as well—wherever there may be conflicts of opinion. Before stating a case before a group, you should: (1) Condition yourself in visual imagery, by testing the techniques described in detail in Chapter 2 and applying whichever one is most appropriate. (2) Having made yourself the focal point, think over what you intend to say or do. (3) Then, through exercises in mind expansion, picture yourself in action. (4) Change action into reaction by picturing yourself as a disinterested listener rather than an intensive speaker. (5) Finally, review the whole process from start to finish, rehearsing yourself for the occasion.

Almost invariably you will find that Step 3, the injection of mind expansion, represents the crux of this technique. At that point you may decide to change your approach entirely, because you find yourself getting out of character; or you may so solidify your original opinion that you will be able to simplify it, or even go for broke on one count alone. If you are torn between two choices, an exercise in dilemma-solving or a reference to such cases can give you the right answer.

Here is a classic example:

Some years back, a man named Staub began as a bricklayer and worked his way up to becoming a building contractor. As such, he proposed a large civic project that required his appearance before the board of aldermen in one of America's largest cities. As he pictured himself stating facts to the board, he began to recognize complex questions that would be in their minds and he realized that he could not begin to answer those of such a large assemblage. All he could do was plant his message and let his listeners take it from there. So he went back to the basic premise of stating his case in fundamental terms so simply and directly that at least one man would fully understand him.

Then he had an inspiration. On a large board there must surely be one man who had been a bricklayer like himself. So he keyed his talk to that imaginary listener, planting only the ideas that a bricklayer would follow through to the point where others could take up the general theme. As he viewed his listeners, he kept turning his gaze to different parts of the hall, briefly reiterating his pointed comments so they wouldn't be missed by the one man for whom he intended them.

The entire board discussed the proposal that same day; the next morning Straub was notified that it had been accepted and would be taken up in detail by a special committee. Afterward, Straub learned from committee members why he had made out so well. There wasn't just one former bricklayer on the board of aldermen: there were five. Wherever Straub had looked, there had been a man who helped sell his plan to the board.

This technique of addressing an entire group by focusing your attention on one member (real or imaginary) ties in directly with earlier comments on stage fright in Chapter 11 in connection with advanced technique in gaining self-confidence before an audience. I purposely reserved its discussion until this point for several reasons: I first wanted to cite Straub's experience to emphasize its main application—as a means of purposeful attainment rather than simply a mechanism to overcome a temporary setback.

An inexperienced speaker, particularly one who either lacks a message or has forgotten it, should use a basic form of confidence-builder before looking for approval from a friendly face, since there is no guarantee that he or she will immediately find one.

But when you are reasonably sure of yourself or are familiar with what you intend to say or do, it is a good plan to individualize your audience from the start, looking from one person to another until you have established your own coterie, so to speak.

That sums up a twofold message in personality development through mental discipline. Don't hem and haw. Rehearse yourself for the part you are to play. Cut out superfluous words and discard any mannerisms that detract from the better self you are trying to create. Try taping yourself on a recorder and play it back while repeating your actions before a mirror.

Study yourself, know yourself, be yourself.

Certainly you are not reading this book to change your personality totally; that would be a kind of emotional murder. Even the present decade's pop psychology fads have not created personality metamorphosis. Indeed the real secret of most such rackets is that human beings herded together tend to be more suggestible as a result of the dynamics of group interaction, especially if there is a charismatic or inspiring leader. There is also less feeling of personal responsibility in large groups, whether they be a football, hockey, or little league game, revival meetings, political rallies, rock concerts, or a vigilante movement. Consequently, when the guru admonishes, badgers, and embarrasses his customers to confess, the paying victim is really coerced to expose and strip himself by his public confession.

Does such a visitor experience a true personality transformation? Not really. He may become motivated by finding a common bond, by being with people who are generally seeking similar aims in taking the course; for example, a search for some other purpose in life, more goals, instant gratification (like winning a lottery), a magic cure for everything, and a way of overcoming loneliness.

The price, however, is an expensive one, for such weekend experiences are temporary. Lasting friendships are not made; a return to home finds the same problems.

The impact of group suggestion—in fact all suggestion—is temporary, unless you have been shown how to reinforce and build upon it. The real tragedy of what could at best be considered an emotional weekend fling is in the shocking realization by the participant that he had days ago exposed himself and his feelings to a plastic group of strangers in an unprofessional atmosphere. Not everyone can handle such a trauma, and the constructive effects of such a shattering ego trip are short-lived and followed by lonely depression.

Today we are told that a salve will remove skin blemishes overnight; that a drug will calm us and all our problems; that we can lose weight by a new formula, even though we eat whenever hungry; that we can build muscles by spending a few seconds a day with a machine that does all the work; and yes, that we can win friends and influence people by changing the frames of our glasses, using a certain razor or hair spray.

The truth is that there is no magic formula, that you and I are the sum total of the various facets of our personalities, with our drives, interests, talents, frustrations, and the multitude of other personal facets which make us a human living being. It is working with these facets that can improve on the whole. By singling out those pluses within you, the talents, skills, or potentials which have not been developed to the fullest, you will be giving yourself a new lease on life. In truth, you want to be what you are—but you want to be better at it. This will require some genuine time and effort on your part, but you're worth the investment. After all, is there anything in life that is worthwhile to use unless we've earned it?

I've seen, through the years, some dramatic improvement in individual life styles, with the individual getting more and more out of each day.

How well I remember the mother who played on a bowling team for years, never playing more than merely average. When she raised her average some 28 points in six weeks she became the center of attraction of her team. Even though she was still quiet and soft-spoken, one could see a greater enthusiasm and communication between her and her playmates.

How many students have found in improving their studies more time to devote to campus activities, rather than the anxiety of endless hours in secluded study simply to avoid flunking out. But there is a bonus beyond the specific aim to which you may put the techniques of suggestion, controlled imagination, and attention that I have taught in these pages—being able to concentrate and to feel an idea, or a series of ideas, more dynamically. You will find a world of feeling and experience around you which so many people through life appreciate only superficially. That's what life is all about. There is a joy and an inner contentment in savoring all of life around you; of that I can assure you, because I've known that joy.

ML